Parenting
With
Patience

Turn frustration into connection with
3 easy steps

Judy Arnall

Library and Archives Canada Cataloguing in Publication

Arnall, Judy, 1960-, author
Parenting with patience : turn frustration into connection
with 3 easy steps / Judy Arnall.

Includes bibliographical references and index.
ISBN 978-0-9780509-5-5 (pbk.)

1. Parenting. 2. Parent and child. I. Title.

HQ755.83.A75 2014   649'.1   C2014-902677-3

Published by Professional Parenting Canada, Calgary, Alberta, Canada

www.professionalparenting.ca

First Edition 2014

Although the author and publisher have exhaustively researched all sources
to ensure the accuracy and completeness of the information contained in this
book, we assume no responsibility for errors, inaccuracies, omissions, or any
other inconsistency herein. Any slights against people or organizations are
unintentional. Readers are strongly encouraged to use their own judgement in
their parenting decisions.

Editing by Jody Amato, www.inkblotcommunications.com

Cover Design by Bobbie-Jo Bergner, Layout Design by Sandra Auriti,
Mind's Design Studio, www.mindsdesign.ca
Illustration by Marlin Arnall

Printed and bound in Canada

Table of Contents

INTRODUCTION

I recall one of my less-than-stellar parenting moments that I wrote about in
Discipline Without Distress; to this day, all my children also remember it. I had
a really bad day. I was under stress. I needed to get a handout ready for a class,
and my printer wasn't working. I had four children under eight years of age. I
was furiously trying to get the printer working when the two younger children
started fighting. I yelled. I fumed. I threatened to put them in their rooms and take
away TV for a week. Completely frustrated, I took a hammer to the printer. The
children were in tears. I was in tears, and the printer wasn't in great shape either.
I felt embarrassed for demonstrating a very poor expression of anger in front of
the children, and I regretted taking away TV for a week. I knew when I calmed
down that the TV punishment would never be enforced. The printer and handout
problems eventually were solved, but the relationship between the children and
I was not repaired as quickly. Now that my kids are older, we laugh about that
incident, which was not one of my prouder parenting moments. Luckily, children's
memories don't start much before four years of age, which is Mother Nature's way
of forgiving parents during those really tough years of parenting small children.
On the flip side, we still have to be careful how we handle stress because children's
brains record what they see, feel, and experience.

Living with other people is joyful, satisfying, and hard work. Because we don't
always agree and we have needs that may conflict with the needs of our partners
and children, strong emotions arise. We feel anger and frustration. It's a normal
part of life and relationships. Anger is one of the hardest things to deal with in the
family because of the perception that families must always be loving. But anger can
also be very productive.

As a wife for 25 years and mom of five children, three of who are now adults, I
found myself getting angry quite a lot in their early years. Sleepless nights, messes,
spills, destroyed items, children who don't listen, feeling unappreciated, and a

rushed schedule can bring out the worst in normally nice people. As children grow, there are fewer and fewer issues to yell about, so parenting school-agers and teens becomes easier. However, parenting is one of the hardest jobs on earth. Parenting requires constantly caring for another person, and staying patient under time pressures is a goal that many parents find difficult to achieve.

As a professional educator who teaches parenting and child development, I resolved to never punish my children and managed to do that for the most part. However, many times I yelled and went off on angry tirades. I threw things and broke a few others. I swore a lot. Thank goodness that no one is perfect.

I teach parents not to use physical punishment and many of us are not doing that any more, yet we resort to yelling and swearing which might be considered a form of emotional punishment. A *New York Times* article even went so far as to say that yelling is the new spanking. (Stout, 2009) A 2003 study published in the *Journal of Marriage and Family* found that parental yelling is quite prolific: of the 991 families interviewed, 90% of them admitted that they shouted, screamed, or yelled at their children at least once in the previous year. (Sutherland-Smith, 2013)

Although sporadic yelling probably doesn't cause children irreparable harm, we don't like it when we behave that way and we really hate it when our children copy us.

We wake up each morning and hope for more patience. At night, we feel tremendous guilt when kissing our sleeping angels goodnight and remembering their scared little faces when we yelled at them during the day. We wonder what happened between the morning and the evening.

As children grow, two things happen; they become much more verbal and able to understand our words and hence "listen" more, and they become much more physically capable of navigating their own needs and lives. Those two factors make parenting much easier and the opportunities for yelling greatly decrease as children age. Patience comes easier.

You are probably reading this book because you don't want to wait until your children are school-aged to have more peace in your home and wish to cut down on the yelling now. Good for you! I hope this short manual helps. The three steps you'll learn have helped many thousands of parents that I've taught in groups and classes.

Start small. Practice just Step 1 for a month and see how much calmer things are. Then try Step 1 and Step 2 in tandem. Then do all three steps. You will be well on your way to more conscious and non-punitive parenting.

Keep in mind that there is no one correct way to parent. There are many, many good ways to parent and a few not-so-good ways. The reason for so much published information about parenting is that no family is the same. A family combines different personalities, values, attitudes, beliefs, temperaments, genders, ages, learning styles, and intelligences; each member has a unique relationship with every other member. With so many variables, it's no wonder there is such a plethora of varying parenting advice. Innumerable dynamics elicit innumerable approaches.

The one thing that unites all family members and differentiates family relationships from those we share with others—neighbours, friends, employers, employees, and colleagues—is that family relationships are love-based relationships and we must treat our family members with care. However, that doesn't mean we feel unconditional loyalty for family members. And just because a person is a family member doesn't mean that we can abuse them or take liberties that we would not take with people outside the family.

You Are a Fabulous Parent!

 "People who get nostalgic about childhood were obviously never children." ~ Bill Watterson, Cartoonist

If you are reading this book, you are a wonderful parent. Please rest assured that your occasional lapses of anger will not wreck your child or destroy his brain development or mess him up for life! If you are a kind, patient parent for about 70% of the time, you are doing well and your child will be absolutely fine. You are human and so are your children; parents all lose it at times. Cut yourself some slack and let go of the guilt.

Stress affects all of our lives, including kids. The three types of stress include positive, tolerable, and toxic stress. In all cases, stress produces cortisol and adrenalin in the body. Stress is felt in the brain and in body responses. (Harvard University, 2014)

Children experience positive stress when preparing for sleep-away camp, looking forward to a birthday party, or studying for an exam. Parents experience positive stress when preparing for a presentation, planning a holiday, or trying a new sport. Positive stress is temporary, builds resiliency, and allows us to feel good about our accomplishments.

Tolerable stress describes a negative, temporary event in a child or parent's life: divorce, a hurricane, a move, or a death of a beloved relative. What makes this type of stress tolerable is that the stressful effects are buffered by at least one caring, loving adult who supports and helps a person through the trauma. The stress eventually subsides and the person withstands the stressful effects.

Toxic stress includes ongoing, prolonged, inescapable, negative events that are not buffered by caring people in our lives. Stress caused by a death in the family, neglect, abuse, addictions, or parents with ongoing mental health problems becomes toxic when a child or parent has no one to talk to or provide support, comfort and care.

The science behind anger and brain development shows that toxic stress affects a child's brain architecture: namely, the ongoing release of cortisol and adrenalin negatively affects neurons. Temporary release of cortisol and adrenalin, as in cases of positive stress, provides motivation and energy. Ongoing release with no cessation, as in cases of toxic stress, can be damaging. It's like a car driving on the highway, in which acceleration is the cortisol and adrenalin. The temporary acceleration used to pass another vehicle is good. Ongoing acceleration is not good and can damage the motor if used too long. The same is true in parenting. For example, if you yelled at your child every day for five hours and she had no one else to turn to, her brain development could be affected by that stress. Children are fine with positive and tolerable stress, which is occasional and not ongoing, and when still buffered by caring adults. Children show amazing resiliency to normal parenting anger. So if you lose it once in a while but are generally a kind and patient parent—which most parents are—you will not inflict long-term brain damage. You are a great parent!

What Every Person Needs to Know About Anger

Let's explore a few facts about anger:

- Anger is a normal, healthy, productive emotion that everyone feels. Anger is a part of the human experience.
- Anger can be neutralized by appropriate or inappropriate behaviours or expression. The more you express your anger, the more it loses its grip on you.
- The ultimate goal of anger is to solve a problem. Anger alerts us to change! This is a good thing.
- Change can be as simple as letting go of the issue and realizing it's not a big deal.
- Or perhaps it is a big deal and you need to make major resolutions and commitment to solving the problem. If you sleep on the issue and are still angry the next day, chances are you can't let it go and need to resolve it.
- We can choose to not give our anger the energy or "gas" it needs to continue.

We choose when to stop anger. We can feel it, express it, and then change what caused it.

- We usually vent anger on those closest to us. Let's face it—our families are safe outlets. They love us no matter what. Unfortunately, they get to experience our anger more than outsiders because we can relax and be our true selves with people we love and trust. Familiarity with family and the safety of home make it easier to be angry there rather than with a peer group, friends, or at work. As my daughter says, "Home is where you go when you can stop being artificially nice to people."

- Others can't make us angry. They do things and we react. We own our anger. Rather than say, "She made me so angry," we need to say, "I felt angry when she..." We take responsibility for feeling and expressing our anger. Anger is all about us and how we react to things. We all have certain buttons that can be pressed, and we need to analyze what it is that makes those buttons hot.

- Anger is often a secondary emotion caused by an unacknowledged first emotion, such as frustration, fear, jealousy, stress, hunger, embarrassment, loss, grief, and sadness. Fatigue, feeling unappreciated, and lack of "me time" are three big ones for parents.

- Anger is hard on the body. It causes the release of stress hormones, such as cortisol and adrenalin, which are beneficial for us in the short term, but endanger our health when sustained long term.

- Anger usually indicates we feel hurt in some way. Reducing our triggers helps to reduce the amount of anger we have to deal with.

- Our homes are living classrooms for learning how to handle anger. As children, we may have been taught how to handle our anger either directly, such as being told to "Use your words!" or indirectly, by watching our parents, TV characters, or even the audience at a hockey game! When you were a child, how did your parents express anger? My parents yelled and swore a lot. I tend to yell a lot and my children do, too.

- Children need to witness healthy expression of anger. They need to see adults use anger productively to make change.

- Unresolved anger will resurface at a later time. Anger management does not mean suppressing anger. It means recognizing it, feeling it, expressing it, and then using it productively to solve the problem.

- Anger and aggression are not the same. Anger can be expressed assertively using I-statements rather than You-statements. It can also be expressed in many other ways.

- Respectful anger does not hurt healthy relationships or people. We choose if and how we vent anger. An expression of anger shows that we care enough about the other person to discuss the issue and have enough confidence in the relationship to reveal our true selves.

- Anger does not reflect badly on the character or personality of others. Being angry does not mean being angry forever. Feelings are fleeting. Like cravings, anger builds, crests, and then subsides. It is only temporary.

- Feeling angry does not always happen when we think it should or when we think we have the right to be. It is as natural as our feet. We don't question why our feet are part of our bodies, so why do we question if we should feel angry about something?

- Anger seems inappropriate only when we don't understand it.

- How we express our anger can trigger or escalate other's anger. We have to be very conscious about that when we express anger.

- When dealing with anger in children, we can't deny our own angry feelings, because then our child's outbursts will trigger ours and we will react with anger. We, as the adult in the situation, need to stay calm and find healthy ways to neutralize our anger in order to help our children with their anger. As adults, we have had more experience with anger and have more self-control techniques built up over time than children do.

- Punishment for expressing feelings, such as anger, can be very disastrous for children and result in the repression of feelings. Repression of feelings can have serious health risks: high blood pressure, depression, stress, worry, addictions, eating disorders, cutting, heart attack, stroke, and many other illnesses.

- Children need to learn to feel, express, and resolve their anger as a genuine life skill. Learning to handle anger productively takes at least the first twelve years of childhood and much repetition.

- Most young children express anger with physical aggression that becomes more frequent by age two, peaks at age three, and then tapers off around four when children become more verbal.

- **The most important point is that anger should not be expressed in any way that hurts ourselves, hurts other people, or hurts our treasured belongings.**

Anger begins in the brain

Anger starts as a perceived hurt or injustice. We misinterpret information or make assumptions.

It can be stopped at this point by asking, "Do I know everything? Is there something that I am missing? Should I ask more questions?" Seek first to understand! Often, additional information reduces anger because we better understand the intent of the other person.

It's very, very difficult to listen to another person's point of view when we are angry. But it's very important to do so, because often we make assumptions before we have all the information.

If your assumptions are incorrect, calm down and be glad that you didn't act out by hurting someone or something. If your assumptions are correct, express your anger without hurting anyone or anything, by asserting yourself with an I-statement, and move on to problem-solving for now or next time.

Anger continues in the body

Anger can cause an accelerated heart rate, heated and flushed cheeks, a burning sensation around body parts, tears, rapid breathing, dry mouth, a throbbing head, racing minds, dizziness, and the body's release of adrenalin, which makes us stronger and energetic. That physical energy must be released in some way.

Typical ways people express anger

- Yelling
- Throwing things, slamming doors, or breaking things
- Threatening a negative or punitive consequence
- Speaking with name calling, attitude, criticism, or sarcasm
- Hitting, spanking, or pushing
- Swearing
- Withdrawing by sulking but hoping someone notices and cares

When stress is high, we respond with our emotions and reactive impulses. When stress is low, we can respond with the thoughtful, reasoning part of our brain.

What's wrong with our typical expressions of anger?

- We model aggression instead of problem-solving.
- We create fear of our reaction. Children, especially, get scared when their mommy or daddy loses it!

- We create mistrust so that our children don't come to us with their problems because they sense we might be angry.

- Our reaction can affect our children's self-esteem and self-confidence when we attack them from our own anger.

- It's not pleasant for the other people around us.

How can we address anger and experience it more productively? There are three simple steps.

Step 1
Get Yourself Calm:
Time-out

STEP 1
GET YOURSELF CALM:
TIME-OUT

Time-out is for You!

One day while making dinner, my four-year-old son, Scott, came up to me and asked if he could have a bag of chips. I said, "No, we are having dinner soon." After much begging, and me denying him the chips, he stormed off to his bedroom. He was very quiet except for a repeated stomping. Because the stomp was occurring so regularly, I went up to see what was going on.

I opened the door to his room. There were broken chips spread all over the white berber carpet. He had opened the bag, in defiance of my declaration, and poured all the chips on the carpet. He was so angry, he then ground every last greasy chip into the carpet, smashing them to ease his anger. Being a very spirited child, he was persistent and didn't finish the job until the last chip was crushed.

Was I angry when I saw this act of defiance? You bet! I was livid! In one of my prouder parenting moments, I followed Step 1 and took a time-out. I was so angry, I was scared I would hurt him if I touched him, so I said in a calm voice, "I am so angry, I can't speak. I need a break." With that, I left and went downstairs to phone my husband and cry. I was taking a time-out to calm myself as the first order of business.

Good parents sometimes feel anger toward their children. It's a basic fact of life. We need to accept that anger is normal in every love relationship, whether with a child, partner, co-worker, or friend. How we deal with the anger can either damage the relationship or make it a valuable source of teaching that strengthens our connection.

Studies show that taking a brief time-out to regain composure is one of the healthiest ways to deal with anger. This is not a lengthy sulking time-out of no talking that is often meant to be punishing, but a short break from the situation. Parenting books stating that deeds must be dealt with in the moment, or children will forget, do not take into account the emotional needs of the child and the parent. (Neufeld, 2004) The anger of the parent and the child must be dealt with first, before the resolution, in order to maintain a calm, rational response.

Good kids get angry, too. It's normal and healthy to feel anger. Part of the job of growing up is to learn how to deal with anger in a way that doesn't hurt anyone or anything. Children need to learn to take ownership and responsibility for their anger and how to make it work for them as an indication that change is necessary. As parents, we can coach them in the job of learning to express anger. It's not the most pleasant job in parenting, but it is one of the most essential. Children who have self-control over their anger will do well in life, jobs, and future relationships.

When we are angry we want others to care that we are angry. Children also feel that way. They want caring shown in the form of hugs, nurturing, soft words, and acknowledgements such as, "That must have been excruciating for you. You are very angry about that experience." They want us to listen, nod and validate their feelings with a sincere response.

Before we can attend to children, we must attend to ourselves. It helps to look at our overall parenting style.

Parenting Styles

"Children are unpredictable. You never know
what inconsistency they're going to catch you in next."
~Franklin P. Adams, Columnist

What is your parenting style? Are you strict or easygoing? Our style determines the parenting challenges that trigger our anger.

We all have different parenting styles. A parenting style is defined as the way a parent consistently behaves the majority of the time toward his or her children. Majority is defined as about 70% of the time. Parents waver from their preferred parenting style when they are sick, under stress, absent or on vacation. They also waver when their children are sick, visiting or other unusual circumstances. The environment also determines wavering of parenting styles. What is tolerated outside may be curtailed inside.

Parenting styles can affect a child's well-being in the areas of:

- Social and emotional competence
- Cognitive development and academic performance
- Physical health
- Problem behaviour

The style used under normal day-to-day conditions dictates the parenting style. For example, a parent's reaction to the following common childhood issues may give a clue to the parent's style.

What is your parenting style? How do you resolve common parenting issues?

Parenting Issue	Authoritarian	Authoritative or Collaborative	Indulgent
Sleep	Leave child alone to cry it out	Problem-solving so everyone is sleeping safely	Sleep with parents but parents awake
Eating	Forced eating	Feeding relationship where parent provides healthy food and child decides quantity	No regular social mealtimes
Discipline	Physical and emotional punishments	Teach and explain	Tolerate bad behaviour
Learning	Forced learning through bribery and punishments	Facilitate learning	Provide no learning supports

Parenting styles quick overview of characteristics

Here is a description of the various parenting styles. Research from many sources shows that when the Authoritative or Collaborative style is used most of the time, the outcomes for children are optimal. The Authoritarian, Indulgent, and Neglectful Styles are associated with poorer outcomes for children. The less punitive the style, the better for the child. (NLSCY, 2002-03)

The Authoritarian parenting style: "It's my way or the highway"

- Parents make most decisions for the child, and sets goals for the child. The child has almost no input.
- Parent's needs are more important than the child's needs.
- Parents make all the rules for the child and the rules are non-negotiable and rigidly enforced.
- Parenting tools used are punishments, and behaviour modification techniques such as reinforcements, extinguishment and ignoring. Tools may include sarcasm, shunning, ridicule and embarrassment. Consequences are logical, or natural and tend to be punitive.
- Children learn that love is highly conditional on their behaviour.
- Children learn what to think instead of how to think, and are easily manipulated.
- Children must obey without question and often comply due to fear of the parent.
- Family life is rigid and very structured.
- Child compliance is valued as more important than a close parent-child relationship.

The Authoritative parenting style: "You can have input, but I will still decide"

- Parents make most of the decisions and sets goals and rules with consideration of the child's input.
- Parent and child needs are equally important and they strive to meet both at the same time, although parent's needs will triumph when true conflict presents itself.
- Enforcement of rules may involve emotional punishments such as parent controlled time-outs, logical consequences, grounding, withdrawal of privileges but usually not physical punishments.
- The parents acknowledge the feelings of the child, but what the parent says still goes.

- Parenting tools are communication skills, negotiating, and problem-solving as well as some behaviour modification techniques such as reinforcement, ignoring, timed time-outs and praise. Logical consequences are constructed to teach the child lessons and might not be solution based; they may be punitive.

- Family life is a balance with structure and flexibility.

- Children are taught how to think in addition to what to think.

- Emphasis is on the relationship rather than compliance, but compliance is still highly sought after.

- The main difference between this style and the collaborative style is that the parent will use emotional punishment with children. Children are still treated differently in comparison to other people such as adults. In the Collaborative style, no punishment is used at all, in the same manner as all other relationships such as neighbors, friends, relatives, employer, and partner. Conflicts are solved as "problems" instead of discipline issues and children are afforded the same respect of their thoughts, feelings, wants and needs as any adult person.

The Collaborative parenting style: "Let's find a win-win solution together"

- Collaborative parenting strives to involve the child's opinions, feelings, and age-appropriate decisions. Parents don't hand the power of parenting over to the child, like giving the child the whole rope, but instead, give the child a longer piece of the rope as the child ages, under the watchful presence and guidance of the parent.

- Parent and child's needs are equally important and they strive to meet both at the same time. The parents set few rules except for safety rules, and almost all rules are negotiable. Rules may not always be enforced, but may be re-negotiated. Enforcement of rules involves solving the problem rather than arbitrary consequences or punishments.

- Parents give their child as much freedom as possible except for physically dangerous situations.

- The parents acknowledge the feelings of the child and works with the child to find solutions acceptable to both.

- Parenting tools are communication skills, problem-solving, natural consequences and facilitation of learning. Natural consequences teach the natural order of life, are "real world" solution-based, and never designed or intended to be punitive in order to "teach a lesson."

- Family life is somewhat structured but parent involvement is high.

- Children are taught how to think, rather than what to think, and are encouraged to brainstorm and problem-solve issues, to a win-win resolution.

- In win-lose type of battles, both the parents and children work together to win-win.
- Emphasis is on relationship building rather than child compliance.
- Children are treated as respectfully as other relationships outside the family.

The Indulgent parenting style: "He can't help it"

- Children receive too many material items and too much of anything that is not healthy in moderation.
- Parents try to shield children from all possible difficult or unpleasant experiences and from natural and logical consequences of their actions. This is also called "Helicopter" or "Snowplow" parenting.
- Parents require no age-appropriate contributions from the child in the form of chores, financial help, educational attainment or employment.
- Rules are rarely enforced and parents give in on most conflicts when the child displays anger from not getting their way.
- Child's love for parents is conditional and they are often treated disrespectfully.
- In power struggles and battles, the child wins most often.
- Emphasis is on making the child happy, rather than building the relationship.

The Uninvolved parenting style: "It's not my problem"

- This style does not require respect or contribution from the child.
- Parents indulge the child and makes few demands when present.
- Parents are as removed as possible from their children's lives. Children get almost no supervision or direction from their parents.
- Parenting tools involves inconsistent bribes, threats, and punishments and emotional and physical unavailability.
- Family life is non-existent. Children and parents may live separate lives but in close physical proximity.
- Children learn that love is conditional.
- Conflicts are not discussed or acknowledged.
- No nurturing, warmth, or comfort is given by parents as no relationship is present.

Parenting styles are rooted in many factors

- The family dynamics in which the parents were raised when they were children.

- The personalities and temperaments of the parents (controlling or easygoing).

- The personalities and temperaments of the children (introvert or extravert, strong-willed or easygoing).

- The moral and religious beliefs of the parents.

- The culture in which the parents were raised and the one they currently are raising children in.

- How much knowledge the parents have about child development and positive parenting practices.

What type of parent are you?

Diana Baumrind researched parenting styles in the 1970s and found three basic types: authoritarian, authoritative, and permissive. These styles captured two elements of parenting, which she called demandingness and responsiveness. According to Baumrind, demandingness is "the claims that parents make on the children to become integrated into the family and community by their maturity expectations, supervision, disciplinary efforts, and willingness to confront a disputative child." Responsiveness is "the extent to which parents intentionally foster individuality and self-assertion by being attuned, supportive, and acquiescent to children's needs and demands." Baumrind continues by saying that authoritative parents are both highly demanding and highly responsive. Authoritarian parents are highly demanding but not responsive. Permissive parents are highly responsive but not demanding. (Baumrind, 1967, 1971)

These styles are based on several criteria, such as goals of the parent, who makes decisions about the child's life, and who makes the rules. Since then, several other philosophies have been introduced, such as "Attachment Parenting," "Free-range Parenting" and the "TCS Movement (Taking Children Seriously)." These philosophies have a high collaborative component between parent and child, and also combine high parental involvement, high parental teaching and guidance, but low parental control. Many of these families have very happy, normally functioning children and would not fit well in Baumrind's model. As well, many authoritarian parents demonstrate a high degree of warmth and nurturing in addition to their expectations and punitive discipline, which also produces well-adjusted children. See the Appendix for "Parents' Quick Guide to Parenting Information" based on these parenting styles.

Almost fifty years later, parenting styles have changed. I propose that there are five distinct styles, which incorporate the same axis but have broader definitions. The two axis points are nurture/warmth/comfort and expectations/structure, replacing Baumrind's responsiveness and demandingness in the Parenting Style Axis. This model is adapted from Baumrind's model and is presented in *The Parenting Information Maze.* (Arnall, 2014)

Personally, I think that nurturing is even more important than structure. The outside world in the form of laws, schools, workplaces, teachers, extended families, and friends all provide structure. But only parents can steadily provide nurturing, listening, comfort, and responsiveness—in essence, unconditional love.

Ideally, parents should strive for the authoritative and collaborative parenting style (upper right) most of the time. This zone incorporates a high level of structure and nurturing. It is impossible to be in this zone all the time, but if parents aim for it 70% of the time, they are doing very well. This style allows for consistency, which is important for children in knowing how predictable their parents are and also allows for times when parents are going to be more authoritative, such as in times when safety is supreme, as well as times parents may be more indulgent, such as holidays and sick days. If parents can totally let go of all punishment, physical and emotional, and practice more collaboration, they will notice much less aggressiveness and verbal pushback from their children. (NLSCY, 2004) (Owens, 2004)

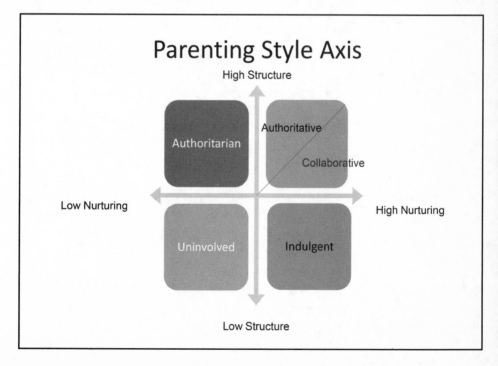

Nurturing/Warmth/Comfort

If structure is like putting on a bandage when a child scrapes her knee, then nurturing is the kiss on the bandage. It's not tangible or measurable in parenting, but it is critically necessary and absolutely noticeable when absent. Families with little nurturing and warmth are reported to have a "coldness" or "perfunctory chill" about them. Nurturing includes physical and emotional affection, kindness, attention, encouragement, support and comfort especially when someone is sick, hurt, or upset. Studies began in the 1950's, most notably, by John Bowlby and Mary Ainsworth, that has consistently proven the validity of attachment, warmth, nurturing and comfort, in the parenting relationship beginning at birth and never ending. (Bowlby, 1988)

Nurturing/Warmth/Comfort checklist

- Expressing unconditional love through kind and encouraging words.
- Providing comfort, care, and attention.
- Listening and giving emotional validation.
- Providing non-sexual touch such as hugs, pats, cuddles, kisses, and stroking.
- Solving all parenting problems without any forms of emotional or physical punishment.

Expectations/Structure

In this model, expectations and structure replaces the word demandingness, which can be quite off-putting to nurturing parents. In reality, everyone has expectations of others in the family, whether spoken or unspoken. Parents have many expectations for their children and work to guide them toward those expectations in the form of established structure. An example of expectations is when some parents expect their children to achieve post-secondary schooling and therefore that expectation guides them to nudge their children to do homework and study.

Expectations must be age-appropriate and geared to the child's temperament, gender, and personality. It helps if parents have some knowledge of child development and understand what to expect socially, emotionally, cognitively, and physically.

Structure is the presence of rules, unspoken and spoken, routines, and consistency of family customs. Structure includes the presence of parent guidance, advice, direction, mentoring, and teaching as well as parental supervision and monitoring of child behaviour even in the teen years. It also includes celebrations, holidays, and activities present in family life.

Expectations/Structure checklist

- Providing for physical, social, academic, and emotional needs.
- Providing or facilitating an education.
- Allowing age-appropriate and child-appropriate decisions and natural consequences when safe.
- Guiding, facilitating, mentoring, coaching, and teaching to navigate life situations.
- Using the collaborative problem-solving method for all conflicts and "discipline" problems.
- Setting family rules and limits together.
- Establishing routines, rituals, and celebrations.
- Providing supervision and monitoring, even through the teen years.
- Holding reasonable, age-appropriate behaviour expectations.
- Addressing bad behaviour without using punishment instead of ignoring or tolerating it.
- Modeling responsible citizenship and relationship skills.
- Expecting the child to live up to all he or she is capable of becoming.

When parents have opposing parenting styles

Parenting can be a real challenge for partners who don't always agree in their parenting styles. Luckily, there are some tips for a more peaceful atmosphere at home.

1. Striving for a united front is difficult.

Let's imagine that you have had two hours sleep and just lost your job. How would you react to your eight-year-old spilling his spaghetti dinner on your new white carpet? Let's also suppose your partner won a half million-dollar lottery and had 14 hours sleep last night. How would he react to the same spillage?

I'm sure that each parent would react very differently to the same behaviour. So why do we expect parents to present a united front to their children? Do both parents have the exact same feelings, stresses, expectations and parenting styles? They don't. Parents are not consistent with each other, nor can they honestly present a united front to their children that would be consistent all the time.

2. Children can handle different ways of doing things.

My son Travis was two-years-old when he learned that when he shopped with Daddy, he had to stay in the cart and sit in the little basket, but when he shopped with Mommy, he could hang off the cart and run around. He never attempted to get out of the cart with Daddy, and always tried with Mommy!

Gender of the parent does make a difference. Moms tend to hold babies facing their chest, and pick up them up to soothe them when they cry. Dads tend to hold babies facing outward as if to say, "Look at the big world you can explore!" and when babies are in distress, dads will pick up and distract. Moms combine child care and play while dads like risk-taking and rough-housing types of play. Moms are more in tune with the child's feelings and can anticipate needs, while dads have to rely on the child to clue them in on what is going on. Moms play the lifeguard role that helps keep children safe, while dads play the cheerleader role that spurs them on to new adventures and encourages them to be all they can. Of course, there are moms and dads who do both roles great, but children thrive even when parents display these different styles. (Barker, 2014)

If any parent has ever tried to explain to their child the different voice tones expected in different environments, they would know that children can handle different expectations. Church voices, playground voices, inside voices, and naptime voices all have different volumes. Children can tell the difference and don't get confused when different environments call for different standards of behaviour. They learn that they can run on the playground and not at church. They can jump on Grandma's sofa because Grandma lets them, but not at home. They always have to clean up the toys at daycare but don't have to at all at Daddy's house, and sometimes have to at Mommy's house. Don't worry that they can become confused. They don't.

3. It's okay to agree to disagree.

Instead of a united front, it's better to create a "supportive team." It's all right to disagree on how things should be handled. There are many right ways to parent and a few wrong ways. Opposing parents can discuss issues and identify the absolute non-negotiable ones in private, and then present their agreed-upon ones to the children. Ideally, this is what should take place. However, what really happens, is that one parent usually doesn't agree but will go along to present the united front to the children. The children can sense this and know there is some wiggle room to work on Mom or Dad; whoever is the parent without 100% buy-in. Children are not dumb. They know when one parent is not being totally honest. It's better for all concerned if both parents are honest with their feelings and viewpoints, but support the parent who feels the strongest about the issue. The parent that feels the strongest will deal with it. Who is this more important for? Who has the strongest feelings? Who can take care of the issue from start to finish?

4. The partner in the trenches is the "expert" about their child.

One thing to keep in mind is that unless a person spends 14 hours a day with a child, they rarely have the insight to know what it entails to parent that long. People who spend little time with children are idealists in their parenting: partners who are away for long periods, friends, relatives, and medical professionals. They may be the experts of parenting that tell you what you 'should' do. Unfortunately, they are not around to hear you say "no" twenty times in a day and only hear the one "yes" you wearily whisper at the end of a long day. They think you are being too permissive. When dealing with children for long hours, you have to take the pragmatist's approach, not the idealist's. You do what works! If you relent, even a small bit at the end of a long day, don't beat yourself up for it! It's okay.

5. There are no perfect parents.

Perfection in parenting is impossible. Do what you can for *most* of the time and you are an excellent parent!

6. What one partner starts, they should finish.

It's not fair to set a punishment on a child and then ask an unwilling partner to support you in carrying it out. If Dad grounds the child, then leaves town on a business trip for two days, is it really fair to ask Mom to carry out the punishment while he is gone? If parents are divorced and living in separate houses, do not expect the other parent to carry out the punishments you have issued. They may not share the same parenting style.

7. Agree on several core values before you have children if possible.

When you became pregnant, chances are you and your partner talked about what you valued and believed in parenting. Try to come up with three core values you share and will work towards. In our family, my husband and I came up with:
   1. No hitting anyone,
   2. Rudeness is not acceptable between anyone regardless of age, and
   3. We agreed we would raise our children at home rather than bring in outside care.
Your family's three parenting core values might be unique to your family.

8. Being supportive of your partner's ruling doesn't mean agreement.

You can state a different viewpoint, but support your partner's choice. Don't undermine him to the children. The key here is to be supportive, not united. Honest communication is preferable. A simple statement to your child, such as, "I don't feel as strongly about the sleepover as your dad does, but his feelings are important to me, and I think you need to go and discuss this with him if you disagree with his decision." Direct the child back to the parent who issued the ruling so they can discuss the protest. Don't you do this. It is not your place to protest on behalf of the child.

If your child is angry that your partner won't budge on the ruling, you can certainly offer comfort and acknowledgement of her feelings without undermining your partner's position. Validate her feelings but also support your partner's authority.

Keep in mind that these eight rules will help to guide both of you toward a more peaceful parenting experience, more honest communication, and less guilt for disagreeing with your parenting partner.

Managing Parents' Anger

 "I'll be right there—just give me one hour. . . "
~Peter Arnall, Parent

All parents, regardless of parenting style, feel anger sometimes with all of their children! It's normal and healthy.

So how do we manage it?

Separate your anger from your discipline (and guilt and worry)

Most parents discipline (teach) or punish (hurt) when they are angry. This is a bad combination because we give a punishment that is very magnified. When children do things that "make us" mad, we want to relieve our hurt and anger, often by hurting them, which may not be the best tool to teach them anything or help them solve problems. It also leaves us feeling very guilty. It's far better if parents separate their anger from discipline measures. We need to take responsibility for our actions when we are angry. Discipline means having the vision to see the long-term picture and keep things in balance. A Chinese proverb teaches, "If you are patient in one moment of anger, you will escape a hundred days of sorrow." It's so much easier to watch what we say in anger than to apologize and try to make amends afterwards.

Relationships are like paper: if you crumple it with lots of hurtful anger and smooth it out, it's never the same clean, smooth piece it once was. So be very careful of what you say in anger. We do have choices and can be conscious of what we say and do.

Why parents feel angry

The reasons parents feel angry are as numerous as there are parents. But number one on the list is, "My child doesn't listen to me." Most children's hearing is fine. What parents really mean is "My child won't do as I ask." This is probably the reason most parents come to discipline classes.

Second on the list is children's deliberate defiance, much like my son's grinding the potato chips into his bedroom carpet. We feel disrespected and a loss of control, even though controlling another human being is next to impossible.

Common parenting issues that trigger anger

- Your child doesn't get permission before doing something.
- Your child doesn't comply with requests.
- Your child's temperament is spirited and they refuse to cooperate.
- Your child's developmental stage is a negative one.
- Your child's personality is a difficult fit with parents.
- The misbehaviour keeps repeating.
- Your children fight and you need them to be quiet.
- Your child throws tantrums after you have said "no."
- Your child hits, screams at, yells at, bites, or pushes a sibling or friend.
- Your child nags you when you are talking on the phone or to a friend or busy with a task.
- Your child purposely breaks an item.
- Your child won't do as you ask in public or while visiting outside the home and you feel embarrassed that your "authority" appears weak.
- Your child talks to you with swear words, attitude, or snarkiness.
- Your children are playing boisterously loud when you are under stress.
- Your child demands something immediately.
- Your child whines and won't stop when you say "no."
- Your child pesters you for attention.

- Your child dawdles or is too slow when you need him to hurry.

- Your child won't talk to you when you ask her a question.

- Your child doesn't share information you need.

- Your child touches something or plays with an item that you've told him not to.

- Your child doesn't do her chores.

- Your child does all or some of the above when you've told him that you are having a bad day and he doesn't seem to care at all.

A low tolerance level for normal childhood behaviours is due to a parent's personality, temperament, background beliefs, religion, culture, and lack of knowledge about child development. It is essential to read an up-to-date brochure from a health clinic, or even better if you are up to it, is a textbook on child development. There is a brief description of child capabilities in Step 2 that might be helpful. We don't get mandatory high school classes on child development even though most people eventually become parents. Just as some people read books about the country that they will be travelling to, reading a book on child development will really help parents to prepare and understand why children behave the way they do.

Knowing that children are naturally messy, noisy, egocentric (self-centered), excited, and clumsy and that they are not just acting that way to get your goat on purpose can really help reframe your anger at their behaviour.

It's important to remember that the above list of common parenting issues details normal children's behaviour that is age-appropriate. Many of these behaviours will go away as children grow, often without any parental intervention.

Do not project ahead!

Parents make the mistake of thinking, "If I don't nip this hitting behaviour in the bud when my child is two, then when she is six, or ten, or fifteen, she will still be hitting others. I have to come down hard now!" Not true! Your child will grow in self-control as her brain matures and will not be hitting as she grows older. Her emotional self-regulation and restraint will improve. (Berk, 2000) Live in the moment. You can relax and address the situation as best and firm but as kind as you can, at her developmental age. Help her handle her anger for just today. She will have lots of opportunities to learn and practice self-control and will find better ways in time to handle her anger and others' anger.

Coping thoughts

Remember that anger begins in the brain. We can rethink and reframe our anger into more positive thoughts. (Arnall, 2012) Below is a list of ways to redirect anger while it's still in your brain and you haven't acted yet. Post this list on your fridge, where you can see it when you start feeling angry:

"It's just a stage. It won't last forever."

"This is natural for this age. He will grow out of it."

"Don't take it seriously. What is the humour in all this?"

"Pick your battles. Is this worth having a tantrum over?"

"This is just the child's natural impulse. She will learn better ways over time."

"This is just my child's coping behaviour. It is not about me personally."

"He can't help it right now. He will get better at it."

"Let's just get though this for now."

"She doesn't have to master self-control this minute. She has twelve years to practice."

"Is this a lesson that he absolutely needs to learn this very day, hour or minute?"

Anger can be caused by other factors than children

- You feel unappreciated for all that you do.

- You are tired, hungry, or thirsty.

- You are scared, worried, and anxious.

- You feel disrespected and unfairly treated.

- Your needs are not being met. You want more understanding, personal time, or sense of accomplishment to feel good about yourself. You've had no downtime recently.

- You're trying to get something done within a tight time frame.

- You have lack of control over how to get a job done.

- You're fed up with daily irritations.

- You have had a few drinks. Try to avoid alcohol. Alcohol lowers a parent's tolerance level.

- You're waiting anywhere: long lines or traffic.

- Your partner is out of town or just got back in town but is still no help.

- You have constant interruptions.
- There are still messes and clutter after cleaning up.
- You feel judged about your parenting when your child misbehaves in a public place.
- You feel rushed. You are trying to multi-task and get too many things done at once.
- You feel stressed. A stressful life, combined with the normal trials and tribulations of parenting, can lead to many angry outbursts. One of the most common ones for parents of young children is getting out the door on time. Instead of yelling, "Hurry up! We are going to be late!" change your attitude to, "That's okay, take the time you need." If you are late, will it really matter five years from now?

Look at your own family of origin and see where your blinds spots are. What triggers your anger and what can you do about it?

Remember the anger acronym

A = Accept it

N = Neutralize the energy

G = Get away

E = Examine why

R = Return and problem-solve

A = Accept that you feel angry and anger is okay

The key is to recognize anger before it escalates. Try and recognize anger in the thinking stage, before it gets to body symptoms. You could try self-talk at this stage. Perhaps there really isn't a problem.

Positive self-talk

We have a choice! Use self-talk to moderate those trigger thoughts that get your anger boiling. About 50,000 thoughts go through our heads in one day. How many of these are negative, unproductive, and bad? How many are positive, optimistic, and cheerful thoughts?

Post this box on your fridge!

Points to remember in the heat of the moment

- It's just a stage. All children go through stages when their behaviour might be hard to deal with. It will pass very shortly. Doing nothing about it means they still will get through it and come out a decent person. They won't go down the path of a slippery slope!

- It's not about you. It's all about the where they are at. Remember her age. It takes 18 years of childhood to get it right. Your child has genuine feelings right now and her behaviour is how she copes with her feelings. It's not about trying to bug you. It's about her. She can't help how she is feeling.

- Look on the brighter side. Someday you will laugh about this or tell your friends about it; maybe even write about it!

N = Neutralize your anger energy in a way that doesn't hurt anybody or wreck anything

Release the energy. It is normal to occasionally become frustrated and angry at our children's behaviour. However, it can be difficult to effectively discipline our children when we are furious. The impulse to give our children a big whack can seem very tempting. The key is to learn anger-management techniques, which enable us to overcome our anger and allows us to use effective discipline later without physical punishment. In this way, not only are we disciplining our children, but we are also teaching them anger-management skills at the same time.

Calm-down Tools

These are immediate things to do in the heat of an angry moment to help you feel the anger and let it go. (Crary, 2003) The same tools are listed in the appendix of this book so you can cut out the boxes and post them where you will see them.

Are you an auditory and verbal person?

- Listen to soothing classical music
- Yell into the toilet and flush your frustration away
- Listen to rock or rap music and dance. Release that anger energy
- Sing your favourite song. It helps to focus on the words
- Talk to a friend. Sharing feelings and talking to another parent or a friend allows you to express feelings and perhaps gain some perspective and insight into handling the situation next time. At the very least, it helps you vent feelings.

- Cry
- Record a tape expressing your feelings. Don't send it to anyone
- Do a three-minute silent scream
- Scream at the wall or in the shower
- Hiss
- Count to ten backwards or forwards. Also try to count to ten while taking slow, deep, deliberate breaths
- Count to ten while drinking a big glass of water

Are you a visual person?

- Watch an aquarium
- Read a book
- Draw pictures
- Visualize yourself in a calm place. See feelings and anger floating away from your body
- Play video or computer games or watch a movie
- Have a white board with the message, "Breathe deeply. Say what you are feeling. Count to ten." This helps with pent-up anger for both parents and kids
- Watch YouTube®

Are you a creative person?

- Write in a journal. Write down your angry feelings and then destroy your notes when you feel calmer. No need for careful word choices. Just write as you feel.
- Make a poster of methods to calm down
- Make a mad-meter out of an arrow and paper plate. Color red, yellow, and green areas on the plate. Post it on the fridge to show everyone how you feel
- Work on a project
- Draw a picture or doodle
- Write poetry
- Write a letter or email but don't send it
- Knit
- Make models
- Play with Lego®
- Play piano or guitar

Are you a self-nurturing person?

- Get a hug
- Take a bubble bath
- Make a calm-down place, a quiet corner or spot with calming devices in it to

help calm down
- Drink from a water bottle
- Eat a snack
- Go out with other people
- Be alone. (This is the traditional child time-out. Look at the many other ways you can teach your child to calm down other than a time-out!)

Are you a physical person?

- Scream into a pillow
- Squeeze stress or hacky-sack balls or oranges
- Play with play dough. Red-coloured Playdough® is best
- Play Lego® or K'NEX® and build a masterpiece
- Clean a room, closet, yard, or vacuum
- Knead bread
- Pull weeds or garden
- Dance, rollerblade, bike, throw and kick a ball or walk
- Shake off feelings
- Breathe in calmness
- Stomp, run, or jump
- Bounce on a handled bouncy ball
- Blow in an anger tube (cardboard paper towel roll)
- Hug—force a smile and a hug— it soon melts into a genuine one and you feel much better in the moment and definitely after!
- Shred or rip paper
- Use a fuss box (a cardboard box you can go and kick the sides in)
- Make faces at the wall
- Beat a drum
- Take a bath or shower
- Play the piano
- Mow the lawn or shovel the walk
- Hit a bop-bag or bean-bag chair, punch pillows, break ice cubes. (Can be frightening to children so use carefully or not in their presence. They will imitate you and may not be as discriminate about what they hit!)
- Hang laundry on a rack or wring towels
- Blow balloons or bubbles
- Do the recycling
- Clean up the clutter and throw it all into one basket
- Take in the bottles for recycling
- Play with toys; your child might join you, and the fun dissipates the anger
- Jump on the treadmill
- Wear a button and touch it when you need patience

Are you a humorous person?

- Make a joke out of the situation
- Read a funny book out loud
- Watch funny videos

G = Get away for a while to think

Gain self-control by taking a parent time-out

For your child's sake, take a break. For all the above situations, think to yourself:

> **Stop—breathe—what do I need?**

If the child is in a safe place, a time-out for parents is a wonderful way to cool off. According to Dr. Gordon Neufeld, author of *Hold On to Your Kids*, there is not enough credible research to show that children have to be punished in the moment or they totally forget later. You can take five or ten minutes to deal with your anger first and calm down, and thus make better, calmer decisions, that will not be punitive, when dealing with your child's misbehaviour. (Neufeld, 2010)

Many parents issue consequences in the heat of anger and when they cool down, they often regret what they said. They know they are never going to follow through, because the consequence is usually pretty exaggerated from the anger. When the parent dismisses the consequence or lessens it, they lose credibility in the eyes of their child. It's better to calm down first, and then think about what is going to happen next before anything gets said.

Go to the bathroom, turn on the shower and yell, "I'm so angry!" If the children are older than ten and you can leave them unsupervised, go for a walk. Go to a bedroom, lie on the bed, close your eyes, and breathe deeply for a few minutes. Take a shower. Time-out for you—try a minute per year of your age!

Avoid giving children time-outs when you are angry

When a parent is angry, the child gets sent to time-out. Honest parents know that the purpose is more for the parent's need to calm down, rather than the child's. This can be isolating and damaging because the child doesn't know why he is in time-out.

It helps to know where your child is cognitively at his age. According to Dr. Otto Weinenger, author of *Time-In Parenting*, children up to seven years of age most often don't know why they are in time-out. They just know that Mommy or Daddy is mad! Even if they know they did something to cause the time-out, they don't have the self-control developed yet to stop doing it. Dr. Weininger states that most children don't have the reflective skills required for time-out, that we may think they do, until age seven. Those reflective skills include the big questions of, "What have I done to be here?" "What was my part in the problem?" "What can I do to make things better?" Those are all questions we hope our timed-out children ask themselves, yet often they are just thinking, "I'm so mad at Mom," "I'm going to get even with my sibling when I get out, and this time I won't get caught," "This is so unfair," and "I hate myself and the whole world." (Weininger, 2002)

When a parent sends a child to time-out, the parent feels stretched to the limit. The parent feels upset because she is unable to control the child. She needs a break from the child and has the power to send the child away. When the child is gone, she can calm down and feel more in control of herself, the child, and the situation. It seems to be working. Parents lose it because they believe they are supposed to be in control. Control is illusionary. There is no such thing as control when another human being is mixed in the equation. Children have their own control. The appearance of control is only maintained by our power as long as the children are little. When they are older and bigger, it becomes a challenge to physically control children. It's very hard to drag and keep a 13-year-old in time-out! It's easier to take a time-out yourself than to force another person to take a time-out.

Problems with sending a child to time-out when you're angry

- The child feels disconnected and banished.
- It teaches that time-out is a punishment and not a valuable life skill.
- It invites power struggles and escalates parent anger when the child won't go to time-out or stay in it.
- It teaches the wrong message; that when someone makes you angry, you can do something to them rather than change yourself.
- It can incite anger, frustration, resentment, rebellion, and retaliation behaviours from the child.
- It can increase sibling animosity when used for sibling conflicts.
- It can be a barrier to parent-child communication.
- Most children need an adult to coach and help them work through their strong feelings, such as anger. They can't do it alone or when they are isolated.
- It's not mutually respectful. Most adults don't want to be banished to a room when they are upset or angry. They want to be noticed, heard and have their

feelings validated, just like children want to be helped.

- Children do not have the necessary reflective skills to understand why they are in time-out until age seven.
- It's embarrassing if done in public and the child is not cooperating.
- It punishes the child for having feelings.
- It models power and not peace.

It is not the adult or "real world" way to solve problems. In adulthood, we can't force another into time-out because of our own anger. We must remove ourselves rather than force the other person to get away from us.

Imagine that you are sitting on a plane. The man behind you begins tapping your seat and it is driving you batty. You ask him to stop and he looks at you and smiles. He keeps on tapping. You are angry. Can you pick him up and drag him to time-out? Not likely. You have two other choices; put up with it and let it go, or move to another seat and get yourself calm. Moving to another seat is the adult way of taking a time-out for yourself to calm down.

The best way to teach a child how to take a time-out when they need cooling down is to model it, rather than force them into it. When a parent models taking a time-out, it's a very powerful teaching tool. It shows children that taking a brief time-out is the grown-up way to get self-control. It's a life skill, not a punishment. Children will copy us and begin to take their time-out willingly.

Ways to take a parent time-out when the child is present

Use your time-outs liberally. We know that when parents are feeling upset, angry, or frustrated over a parenting issue or their children's behaviour, it can help to diffuse the situation if the parents remove themselves to get calm and centered, rather than force the isolation of their child in a child time-out. Sometimes with young children, who are frantically clinging on, this is easier said than done!

Many parents object to the parent time-out; they complain that their small children just follow them, screaming, whining, and complaining. How true! Children are often scared of their parents' distress and follow them for assurances that things are okay. Children need physical security and proximity at these moments but parents often need to be alone to cool off, which can lead to a conflict of needs. There are ways to meet both the parents' and child's needs. Here are some tips to be physically present for small children's needs, but mentally take a time-out for your needs:

- Throw a CD on the stereo and dance hard!

- Use an MP3 player filled with your favourite songs to distract you.

- Have earplugs everywhere: in the car, kitchen, purse, and bathroom. They take the edge off a child's screaming that can damage your ears.

- Lock yourself in the bathroom. Tell the children that you love them, and Mommy or Daddy is feeling angry and needs to take a time-out. Turn on the fan or shower so you can't hear the children, and breathe slowly. Visualize yourself in a calm place.

- Do the Hokey-pokey, and shake it out! Smile and make funny noises and soon you will all be laughing.

- Phone a friend for a brief conversation. Tell her how you feel. Call from the closet or a bathroom if you have to.

- Distract yourself with a magazine.

- Drop everything, dress your children and yourself for the weather, put them in the stroller if needed and go for a brief walk outside. Exercise, fresh air, peace and quiet are wonderful for the soul. Children will be distracted by the sights and sounds and you can think about your anger in peace.

- Play a children's DVD or one of your favourite movies. It will distract you or your child, and give both of you time to calm down.

- If you are in the car, pull into to a parking lot or other safe place. Get out of the car, leave the children in there, and walk around the car twenty times. Cry, breathe deeply, vent, or stomp. Get back in the car when you have calmed down.

- Imagine a soundproof, gentle, clear shell surrounding you and protecting you from screaming children.

- Sit on the porch, find a closet, basement, or somewhere you can be alone. Make sure the children are in a safe place.

- Give your child some toys on the bathroom floor, and take a shower.

- Put your baby in a crib with some toys.

- Tell your child that you both need a group hug. It can be very hard to hug someone you feel angry with, but touch is soothing and helps to heal anger. This works well for some people.

- Use self-talk. Say over and over to yourself, "My child is not trying to bug me right now. She is coping with her strong feelings in the only way she knows how. But I have to take care of me first."

- Remember the phrase: "Get myself calm, get my child calm, and then solve the problem."

What skills do you use to calm down in situations other than parenting? Use some of those strategies if you can. Just as the oxygen masks in airplanes are meant to be used by adults first, so they can be in a position to help the children, you must take care of your needs first when you are angry. The bonus gift is that you are truly modeling for your child how to take a calming time-out when situations become overwhelming. Modeling by example, instead of forcing them into a time-out, is the best way for children to learn self-calming tools.

Dads have their own special ways to take a time-out. Many dads have a "man-cave" in the basement or garage that have calm-down tools such as music, big screen TVs, or hobby equipment. My husband would often take a time-out by mowing the grass. He ran the lawnmower so he could physically express his anger and not have to listen to anyone. Three hours later, he was calm and the grass was merely one centimetre high.

Ways to diffuse anger while travelling in a vehicle

- Driving while angry is a distraction and dangerous. Don't do it.
- Pull the car over and step outside.
- Breathe fresh air—know your children are watching you.
- Stomp your feet outside the vehicle until you feel better.
- Put the car radio on and sing.
- Earplugs in the car help you focus and get centered.
- Stop the car and go home. Leave the children at home with a babysitter or your partner. Go back later to finish the errand.

E = Examine and clarify the reasons you feel angry

Identify your primary feeling. Anger is a secondary emotion caused by a primary one. Ask yourself if you're actually angry with yourself or someone else and taking it out on the children. Sure you feel angry, but what's underneath that? What is the real feeling or issue?

Most often, the primary feeling is lack of appreciation and respect. Keeping score of how you are treated compared to how someone else is treated can also fuel anger.

Some other primary feelings for parent anger

- Fear—your son gets lost in a store.
- Tiredness—you spot a mess in the kitchen left for you to clean up.

- Stress—you have a report deadline.

- Loss —your wedding ring accidentally gets flushed down the toilet.

- Jealousy—your husband visits his mother on your anniversary.

- Hurt—you go through a lot of trouble for a birthday party that your child didn't enjoy.

- Embarrassment—you want the children to behave in front of the boss when you have to bring them to work.

- Disappointment—a special event was cancelled.

- Frustration—daily irritations build up.

R = Return to the person or situation and solve the problem directly

After you feel, express, and neutralize your anger, you're feeling much calmer. You are in control of your feelings and take responsibility for them. Now you can use that anger to solve the problem. It helps to summarize and discuss the problem using I-statements. For example, "I feel angry when I'm rushing to get out the door and my son dawdles when getting ready." This helps clarify what the real issue is.

Now you have three paths to take in resolving the issue. In life, everybody has only three ways to solve any problem. Teach children early that they have three choices and how to execute them. Age five is a good time as they can begin to understand consequences.

- Surrender—let it go.

- Leave—get away.

- Negotiate, discuss, collaborate or compromise and solve the problem.

Let's examine these options.

Surrender

Choosing to do nothing is still a choice; perhaps you are not going to react to the bait this time. If you choose to let it go, stop thinking about it. Ignore it. You are not defaulting to letting it go, but actively choosing this path. You are making this choice for you. Many times, we go over and over the anger situation in our heads. Our thoughts tend to escalate the anger as we rehearse and recycle them. Push those thoughts out. Resolve to not "give it gas" and let it go. Think of a color or object or something else whenever the situation pops in your head. When your mind returns to it, say to yourself, "Blue!" and concentrate on the color or object until you are distracted by something else.

Sometimes we can push thoughts away during the daytime hours when we are busy. However, it catches up with us the minute we put our head on a pillow. Recurring thoughts of anger keeps us from sleeping. That would be a good time to try one of the calm-down tools to get it out of our heads. Get up and write down your anger thoughts. Or, perhaps, have a chat with a friend by instant message. Talk out your feelings. Remember that anger magnifies at night. Issues look very different after you get some rest and it's daytime. Get it out of your system at night, but don't send anyone anything until you look at it with clear eyes in the morning.

Leave

Stand tall and proud; then leave. Walking away from a situation does not mean you are chicken or a pushover. It means you have made a conscious decision to not let that person, behaviour, or situation bother you for the time being. Walking away doesn't mean that you won't come back and address the behaviour later. It is consciously giving the situation time. In the case of small children, you can leave, while still being present, by taking a time-out with children underfoot (see the section "Ways to take a parent time-out when the child is present.")

Negotiate

If you choose not to let it go and you want to take action, choose problem-solving. Problem-solving is also called collaboration, compromise, discussion, and conversing. Brainstorm some options on how you could handle it. Ask for a friend's help in choosing which option would be most respectful and helpful. Then choose the solution and implement it. If your anger involves another person, such as a partner or child, ask them to brainstorm solutions with you in helping to solve the mutual problem.

Remember to plan ahead for handling anger

Plan for next time. Find what works for you. Make an anger coping kit: put in a MP3 player, earplugs, a "Stop!" card, a new DVD you have been meaning to watch, and whatever else calms or distracts you. Or write a new calm-down tool in big letters on a sticky note or piece of paper on the fridge for you to grab the next time you are angry. Some parents ask their children to hold up a yellow (caution color) piece of paper as a signal they are getting frightened by the parent's anger. Keep trying various calm-down tools until you have a few reliable ones that work for you and your child in a hurry. A planned anger response helps parents stay in control.

This is also great for the children to see. They will learn a controlled reaction when handling their own anger by watching your example. If you react badly, don't worry. We are not perfect. Apologize and try again. This is work in progress and will always need fine-tuning.

Tips for breaking the yelling habit

- Ask your children to help you regroup. They could give you a signal that reminds you that you are yelling.
- Put a mirror on the fridge so you can see what you look like when you yell.
- Leave the room, count to 10 or 1,000, and calm yourself.
- If your children are older, walk around the block.
- Try breathing out. You will have less air to yell with.
- Practice getting up and speaking to the children instead of yelling from another room.
- Yell into the toilet and flush away the anger.
- Get a cold with laryngitis. This will force you not to yell!

Choosing to not hit or hurt

Some parents say they "just lose it," but I truly believe they choose to act out "how" they lose it. We can all choose to "lose it" or "get a grip." There is immediate gratification for our physiological selves when we release angry feelings and really let someone have it. It feels better, but only in the short term. Chances are that the outburst has damaged or destroyed a part of a relationship without getting at the real problem. Often, the primary feeling is one where we feel overworked, and unappreciated.

Sometimes it can be difficult to resist spanking children. Sometimes it seems that they are deliberately misbehaving just to annoy us. Sometimes they act up the most when we are rushed, doing something critical, or at an event where we most want them to behave nicely. Often children can feel your anxiety vibes and it makes them anxious. They react by behaving in ways we wish they wouldn't. It's a vicious cycle! We need to recognize both parent and child anxiety and take steps to reduce it. The best method is to walk away and take a brief parent time-out. You will feel so much better when you do!

Research shows that there are many risks to a child's emotional and physical health from using physical punishment. (Gershoff, 2002) There is no research that shows it adds to their optimum health. There is even some link between spanking and children's IQ scores. Parents who spank can affect their children's future educational success because the stress of physical punishment can affect developing brain neurons. (Roan, 2009)

As a parent, there were many times I really wanted to hit my child. Deep in my subconscious, I knew that as a parent educator I shouldn't be doing things that I teach parents not to. How could I give workshops on handling anger when I wasn't practicing what I preach? Those thoughts were going through my head even in the midst of extreme anger. Those thoughts helped me choose to not hit. Every parent can choose their thoughts and commit to not hitting their children.

I also knew that hitting is an easy way to handle frustration in the moment, and can become a common habit. So I always avoided the first hit. It's almost as if one hit was too many and 20,000 would never be enough. I had to choose and promise myself never to do the first spank. I have been proud raising five children without slapping, hitting, or spanking any of them (well, except for once; but don't we all try things once?) They are a varied lot of personality and temperament too. Research shows that many parents raise caring, responsible, and well-disciplined children without ever hitting them. (Gershoff, 2002) If hitting is not necessary to raise children, then why do it?

The added bonus of choosing to not hit is that I don't have to deal with guilt afterward. With guilt comes compensation, and that's where parents fall down in the punishment arena. They hit, feel guilty, and then over-compensate with gifts, privileges, and more "Yes" replies than they really wish to say. It's better to use respectful, non-punitive, teaching, discipline methods in the first place. It results in more consistent parent reactions for the children.

After you are calm and in control, you are in a position to carefully consider the behaviour that irritated you so much and decide upon an appropriate disciplinary response that will teach the child and be respectful.

Shaken baby-child syndrome

Everyone needs to know the difference between systematic "leaving baby to cry it out on a regular basis" and "I'm going nuts and am going to throttle this baby if I don't get a break right now!" Sometimes babies and toddlers have days that seem to test your patience. They have crying days and you try anything and everything to stop it and it doesn't stop. Do not shake, hit or hurt them! Put them in a safe place and take care of yourself and your needs first.

Don't worry about wrecking them! An isolated incident of leaving the baby or toddler to cry for ten minutes isn't going to hurt if you are loving and attentive most of the time. On those bad days, you need some tender loving care right away. It's better to make a safe choice and leave the baby or toddler in the crib or a safe place and get a grip on your emotions. If your child is older, leave him where he is and give yourself a time-out. Get yourself calm first!

How to Get More Patience

Like in a good marriage, it really helps to ignore a lot of daily irritations with children. Anger is like a fish hook. We can choose to bite or swim on by. Sometimes we just keep on swimming! Sometimes we have to ignore the dishes in the sink, clothes on the floor, and books strewn about, or we will be constantly criticizing someone for it.

Patience is a learned skill. We all have varying levels of patience, but we need to learn how to extend it for longer periods and how to loan it to our children. Part of increasing our patience is to learn about child development and understand that much of what our child does is normal behaviour. Learning to handle things that set us off is part of developing that patience muscle. Parents who are home full time wonder how they have so much patience with the children all day, but when they hand the children over to a partner who has only been home half an hour, that individual loses it so quickly. The partner just returning home doesn't have the same patience level because he hasn't had practice developing and using it all day.

- Breathe often!
- Set a time limit. Say, "For the next half hour, I will be patient." Extend your time limit as your patience muscles get stronger.
- See the good intent of others. They are not trying to bug you. It's not about you; it's all about them. Children are born egocentric and learn about others as they grow.
- Live in the present. Forget about the future and all that needs to be done. Don't project ahead. Your child will not be the same years from now, and neither will you. Your relationship will grow and they will listen more, especially if you don't punish them now.
- Relish what is happening now. When you are more patient, things get done more efficiently, even if it's at a later time.
- Prepare for delays. Carry around a good book or something to do that is satisfying for you when waiting for others.
- For traffic tie-ups, listen to a gripping audio book.

- Keep your perspective. Has anyone died because of this roadblock? Will it really matter a year from now?

- Be grateful. When you are delayed, think of all the people you are grateful for. Carry around a notebook in your purse and write a short note to tell them what you appreciate about them. This helps put you in a much better mood. Once a week, stick the notes into envelopes and mail them. Your loved ones will be thrilled.

- Have quiet time every day. Take ten minutes on the front step admiring nature or five minutes in the shower. Even for school-aged children, remove yourself for a half hour and savour the quietness. Be sure younger children are engaged in an activity and safe. You can have a few minutes alone. Hooray for the DVD player!

- Have a time-out room for you! Make it inviting, soothing, and calming. A bedroom with crystals, a water feature, stereo with spa or massage music, candles, calming artwork, plants, books, and cozy pillows can be a welcoming, relaxing room in which to have a peaceful moment. If you have a TV or computer in your room, cover it with a white sheet, so it doesn't remind you of work to be done.

- Avoid multitasking. Living a more peaceful, patient life means taking one thing at a time and at a slower pace. Doing multiple things causes stress and hurriedness, which feeds itself with the frenzy.

- Take your "level of acceptance" to the ground. Accept all and everything! Say "yes" to your children as much as possible, especially to entertain themselves, and you can have some time to do what you want to do.

- Take a course so you have to get out of the house regularly.

- Have a standing order to go to the movies. My friend goes to a first-run movie every Friday night by herself.

- Go to bed at the same time as the kids and get up before they do, so you have your "me time" in the early morning and don't have to fight for it at night when you are tired and much less patient.

- Lock the bathroom door and take a shower.

- Go to a bookstore, coffee shop, or for a quick walk as soon as your parenting partner gets home.

- Accept the many areas in which parents must leave change up to the child. Parents can facilitate change but can't force it. Parents can't control their child's eating, sleeping, toileting, pace, learning, thoughts, feelings, beliefs, values, attitude, personality, or temperament.

Children can't help being children, at least until they grow into their teens

Almost all children from all cultures have the following normal characteristics. Most of these peak around age four when children start outgrowing their egocentric and self-focused centeredness and become more aware of others as they grow. We shouldn't feel angry at children for being children; it's unrealistic to expect adult behaviour from them.

- When children begin logical thinking around age six, they can understand other people's feelings.
- Children can put themselves in danger, as their curiosity grows faster than their body or brain development.
- Children are learning all the time and are exceptionally curious.
- Children are naturally messy and don't know how to clean up.
- Children are naturally noisy, boisterous, and excitable. They don't know how loud they are.
- Children are naturally shy in groups.
- Children all want to feel big, proud, and important.
- Children have their own dream world.
- Children are naturally very active until about age 12 and need bursts of physical stimulation between quiet times.
- Children are not time-focused; they operate at their own pace, not in the hurry-up world of their parents.
- Children have conflicts with things, people, and situations, just like any other person on the earth.
- Children naturally want to please those people they love.
- Children are spontaneous and do things without thinking.
- Children are completely honest.

Parents have the adult role. Part of the adult role in parenting is leadership. Good leaders model appropriate skills. Yes, we are human, but being parents, we try to be better at patience every day that we wake up. If we demonstrate patience, our children will be patient with us and their siblings. They are watching us. Keep at it and pat yourself on the back for every minute of success!

The really, really, really bad days

If you are like most parents and occasionally have a really bad day, don't beat yourself up with guilt. Try asking yourself, "What do we all really need right now?" Nourishment for the body? Get some sleep, exercise, fresh air, or a bath. Nourishment for the mind? Read e-mail, social media, a newspaper, book, or go to a movie. Nourishment for the spirit? Harness some chocolate, aromatherapy, talk with a friend, or take a walk.

A snack, nap, drive, fresh air, or a new activity helps change everyone's mood and the atmosphere of the day. Every parent has bad days. Have a "bad-day plan" ahead of time. Never mind the endless list of things that need to get done. Going to bed knowing that you held your temper and your relationships are intact is much more satisfying than folded laundry and a clean house. Tomorrow is a new day and the chores will get done. Focus today on your relationships and you will have few regrets tomorrow.

Apologizing for mistakes

Okay, we are human. When we slip up, like that day I took a hammer to my printer, we need to address the situation, rather than let it go. I went to the children and said, "I'm sorry for slamming the printer and I broke the house rule. Mommy made a big mistake, and I'm very sorry for doing that."

Then I explained what I should have done instead. "I should have used my words instead of the hammer. Or I could have gone for a walk, taken a deep breath, or got a drink of water. I know that I should have taken a break. Can you think of anything else I could have done?"

Parenting blind spots

We need to be aware of our blinds spots. Little quirks we carry forward from our childhoods are sensitive areas for us. We make mountains out of molehills. As a child, I was often shifted quickly, without time to gather my stuff. My parents would decide suddenly to go home in the middle of the night while camping. I would subsequently lose things and be very upset.

Now, as an adult, losing things is very hard for me. When my children lose things, as all children do, I become more upset over the lost item than they do. My anger is blown out of proportion, and it helps me keep perspective if I know where that quirk is coming from. I have to make a conscious effort to not react.

Just remember, every human, parent, and child feels anger and it is a positive emotion—it alerts us to change our situation. Embrace your anger and handle it with care!

Top 10 phrases to instantly be a calmer parent

Many times as parents, we blurt out phrases that we heard as children and later vowed to never say to our own children. However, that is easier said than done. In times of stress, we revert very easily back to phrases and actions we heard and saw when we were parented.

Parenting skills are learned skills, and we can consciously effect change if we become aware of what needs to be changed. Here are 10 common parenting phrases and 10 alternatives for what to say instead, to nurture closer, caring, and more respectful relationships with our children.

Instead of:	Try:
You are a bad boy!	What did you learn from this? What can you try next time?
Hurry up! We are late!	It's okay. Take the time you need… (vow next time to leave more time!)
Oh NO! Fudge! Look at what you have done!	It really won't matter five years from now! I will show you how to fix this…
You need to…	I need you to…
Because I said so!	I'll explain my reasoning in five minutes when I'm not distracted so much.
Stop that tantrum right now!	You feel frustrated and angry. Can I give you a hug?
No!	I can see you really want that but I can't provide it right now.
You've wrecked my….	I'm really angry right now. I need to take a time-out.
Stop doing that!	Would you consider this?
Suck it up and stop crying.	It's okay to cry and feel your feelings. Want a hug?
Go play and leave me alone.	I love you!

Try any of these substitutions today and you will see how much better your parent-child relationship will be. If you are not sure what to say and how to say it, especially in the moment, don't say anything and just offer a hug. You will be surprised how much body language can communicate empathy and affection, and then you can get on with solving the problem with your child.

Now you are calm. Congratulations! The next step on the way to solving the problem, is helping your children get calm.

Step 2
Get Your Child Calm:
Time-in

STEP 2
GET YOUR CHILD CALM:
TIME-IN

Time-in is for Your Child

Let's go back to the chip story. My son, Scott, whom I had denied potato chips before dinner, was angry with me and crunched all the chips into his carpet.

Scott shared a room with his older brother, who was seven. When the older brother saw the chips grinded into his carpet, he became angry and confronted his brother. Now they were both angry and fighting with their words and hands.

I came upstairs, calm from speaking with my husband. I now had a boost of self-control, which was good because now I had to help my sons get self-control. After I calmed down, I needed to help my kids get calmed down. A "jail-time" time-out for them would have escalated the situation by increasing their anger toward me and each other. They needed time-in with me.

I pulled them physically apart so they wouldn't continue physically hurting each other. I grabbed each by the arm and we went to sit down on the couch. I put a video on the player, and we sat on the couch in silence while the TV distracted the children and they calmed down. Often, I vary this calm-down tool with the "reading out loud" one. I grab a children's picture book and read it out loud amidst the children's crying. Eventually, they would stop crying and begin to focus on the book and start listening. It might take ten minutes, but it is time worth spending. It gives me some reading time, builds their literacy and takes their minds off their anger long enough so they can calm down. We could have used other methods such as breathing, going for a walk, or getting a drink of water; that are listed in the calm-down tool section in Step 1.

When the crying, screaming, and sobbing stopped, we were calm. Now we could move into step 3, problem-solving. But first, let's examine step 2; getting our children calm.

A journalist once asked me, "How do you do a 'time-in'?" Time-in is not some new discipline technique used to punish children. It's a very natural act of comfort and compassion. When we are upset, we often want comfort, not judgement. The same is true with children. They want understanding and all a time-in is about is lending comfort, presence, and empathy to an upset child.

Doesn't time-in "reward" misbehaviour?

This is a common question that I get in parent classes. The answer is "No." Spending time with a child to help them calm down doesn't reward him for his strong feelings. Feelings are uncontrollable - he can't stop them. They are going to come, no matter what you do. He needs an adult's help to limit his behaviours resulting from his feelings.

Getting a child to calm down by hugs, reading, or some other calm-down tool has one purpose only; to get everyone calm. Then the teaching can start. Unless the time spent with the child is the ONLY concentrated focused time they have with parents or loved ones, children will not act up or feel angry in order to get parent's attention.

When we see a child struggling with multiplication, we don't send him to his room with a math textbook and say, "Come out when you know how to do it." Instead, we would sit with him and help him work out the math problems. Yet, when we see a child struggling to contain his emotions, our first response is often to send him to isolation to "work it out on his own, and come back when he is ready," and this is not helpful. Just like math, children need an adult's help to learn how to manage his strong feelings.

Dealing with an angry child

From happiness, sadness, and anger, children feel a whole range of emotions. Which are easy to accept? Joy, excitement, or happiness? Which are harder to accept? Anger, frustration, or disappointment? We feel bad for our children when other people and circumstances trigger these feelings in our children. We feel even worse when we are the source. Anger directed at us is very hard for us to deal with calmly and respectfully.

We don't have many role models showing adults handling children's anger. Most often, we handle it the way our parents handled it. There are not many images of angry parents in TV and other media. When we do see images of angry adults, they are often portrayed as sarcastic or aggressive. We also don't know how to handle our children's anger toward their siblings. How do we feel when our son expresses anger to our daughter? We logically know that our children will be angry at times, but we want them to be loving, too. Often, we are at a loss for how to deal with fighting siblings or playmates.

We are not responsible for their anger (even if they think we are)

The one key that parents have to remember is they are not responsible for their child's anger, happiness, or other feelings. We can facilitate a happy, calm, loving environment, but the child still chooses how to feel. It's unrealistic to expect happy children all the time. We can get into a trap of spoiling them to ensure they are never sad, disappointed, or hurt, but this does our child a disservice. It's called "helicopter parenting" or "snow-plow parenting" when a parent goes out of her way to protect her child from feeling bad. The mad rush for the holiday "must-have" toy is rooted in our desire to keep children from being angry or disappointed. Our job as parents is to help our children deal with their uncomfortable feelings, not protect against them. This is intense in the early years and requires a lot of facilitation on the part of the parent, by showing children how to cope with anger and frustration.

When children learn to handle their anger, they learn a life skill. It takes a lot of time and practice, but they do gradually do it. The rewards are evident when you watch your teenager handle his anger by taking a self-imposed time-out and coming back later to use his best "I-statement" even to you! Tantrums are very normal and age-appropriate for young children. Again, our job is not to prevent them, but help them handle them.

Aggression in Young Children is Normal

Richard Tremblay, who holds the Canadian Research Chair in child development at the University of Montreal, says in his study of 2,000 children, more than 90% of the mothers of seventeen-month olds reported their toddlers were physically aggressive toward others. Children with siblings demonstrated this behaviour earlier. (Tremblay, 2005) The *Globe and Mail* reports that toddlerhood is one of the most aggressive stages in human development and 95% of children grow out of it. They become less aggressive as they learn to delay gratification, use their words, and problem-solve social issues. However, in homes with negative (punitive) parenting, children learn to be less aggressive later than normal. (McGinn, 2011)

Some toddlers are more aggressive than others, but this is not just a factor of parent modeling. Tremblay indicates other factors:

Temperament: Spirited children put more energy into getting what they want and can be more aggressive.

Frustration: Tiredness, hunger, and anger stimulate aggression.

Parent punishment: If toddlers are spanked, they are more likely to hit others.

Parent style: Ignoring a baby's cry and becoming angry with a baby is linked to aggression.

Sibling conflict management: Conflict is normal and can be reduced by certain parenting strategies.

Suggestions for handling aggression

You are enjoying a pleasant coffee and a chat with your best friend, when suddenly your toddler whacks your friend's toddler with a toy truck. There is wailing from the startled child and a stunned, embarrassed silence from the parents around the cafe. All eyes are on you; what are you going to do? What can you do that is respectful, immediate, and teaches your child proper behaviour?

First, recognize that whining, hitting, pushing, and biting are pretty normal behaviours in children aged one to four. They are trying to get their needs met, whether for attention, personal boundary space, or that super interesting toy they've been eyeing. It is no reflection of you or your parenting style.

The problem is that their verbal skills are still very limited and they resort to body language to communicate how they feel, and what they need and want. Our role as parents is to discourage their unsociable methods and encourage the polite methods to get what they want. That means we have to "give them the words" to use, back it by taking action, and repeat it often!

Whining

- Ignore it until they stop.
- Tell them to say it again using their "normal" voice.
- Model the "normal voice."
- Give the desired item instantly when the normal voice is used.
- When in a peaceful moment, ask for "inside, outside, whining, church, and normal" voices so they can tell the difference in voice tone, pitch, and variety.
- Pat your head and pretend you can't hear the "reception" when the tone is whiny. Pretend that interference clears when the request is less whiny.

Hitting, pushing, biting, and throwing

Of course, your first order of business is to apply first aid and comfort to the injured child. Then you need to address the attacker. Not all these suggestions will work all the time, but you need a lot of tools in your toolbox. Try some individually or a combination:

- Determine the attacker's need. Does she want the toy, more personal space, attention, a reaction, revenge or choices? Ask her. Tell her how to ask for what she wants. Use simple words.
- Make eye contact.
- Say "Ouch! Hitting, biting, and pushing hurts!" or "I don't like that!"
- Don't expect sharing until age three.
- Restrain your child in your lap or carry him away to another space to calm down with you.
- Rocking your child or rubbing her back and using a soft, repetitive voice helps your child to calm down.
- Show disapproval in body and facial language and your voice tone.
- Save your loud and sharp "No!" for times like hitting and for safety or emergency situations.
- Have toys and space to redirect your child to.
- Actively listen: "You're frustrated that he grabbed the toy? You want your toy back? We can't hit, but we can ask to have the toy back."
- Teach your child to put up her hand to ward off space invaders.
- Teach I-statements: "I don't like that." "I want the toy." "I'm not done."
- Allow your child his own time to give up a toy. Gently remind him that someone is waiting, but don't force him to give it up. Let him choose when.
- Instead of always saying, "Hurry-up," you could try, "Take the time you need."
- Meeting your child's needs encourages her to think about other's needs.
- Supervise.
- Say "Ouch, that hurt Mommy!" when they bite or hit, and put them down and walk away.
- Teach your child to walk away from annoying situations.
- Say "No! We don't bite. Biting hurts."
- Dramatize your pain and sorrow, so the child knows that you are truly disappointed.

- Give your child something else to bite. "People are not for biting. Here, bite this."

- Remove your child from the situation, but don't banish your child to a room alone. Sit with your child to help her calm down.

- Teach "breathing," "the silent scream," and "stamping feet" when your child is angry.

- Teach "trading" and "taking turns."

- Stay calm yourself.

- Don't grab toys from your child. Model the behaviour you want. Ask for the toy and wait for his consent. Always ask to use things that belong to your child.

- Apologize for your child to the victim, to model what you want to see her do in the future.

- Tell the other child that your child needs space but doesn't have the words to say so yet, so could the other child please give him some room.

- Shower the victim with attention. Have the victim repeat the rule of "no hitting—hitting hurts" to the attacker. Remove the victim and take her with you to do something else. Be sure to increase the attention to the attacker in peaceful times. Show him positive ways to get attention.

- Increase one-on-one time with the attacker.

- If hitting between two children repeats, find something else for one child to do and separate them.

- Acknowledge the feelings of each sibling or child and repeat it for the other child to hear, so she can start to learn empathy and conflicting points of view.

- If hitting repeats, children may be hungry, bored, or tired. Fix the underlying reason.

- Model politeness. Use "please," "thank you," and "no thanks" with your children.

Discouraging aggression

- Limit media exposure.

- Model gentleness. Don't throw, hit, or bite back.

- Step in when play conflicts escalate. Don't ignore it. Children need to learn how to deal with it at toddler, preschooler and early school-age levels.

- Teach problem-solving and calm-down tools.

- Provide healthy outlets for rambunctiousness.

- Acknowledge when children are cooperative with each other.

Some toddlers learn these skills faster and easier than others. Be patient. They need a lot of repetition and practice. After all, that's what childhood is for!

Why do toddlers and preschoolers hit?

Where does aggression come from? Actually, it is in our genes. We evolved from hominids who could fight and defend their lives, territory, and loved ones, and they passed on the ability to survive through aggression to the next generation. Even newborns feel anger when they need something. In addition, in the later half of a child's first year, he demonstrates what is called exploratory aggression—curiosity pushes him to see what reaction hitting or pushing another animal or child will bring. By toddlerhood, ages one to four years, aggression is at its peak. Ages two and three are the worst peak years, when one out of every four interactions between a child and someone else is physical. This is almost every hour! (Tremblay, 2005)

Does nurture or nature affect the amount of level of aggression in a child? Let's pretend that a human is like a car. Aggression is like the acceleration of a car. We all feel aggression. Self-control is like the brakes. We all have braking ability, too, but in varying amounts. Some people have more acceleration and some people have more braking power, also called a developed executive function.

Aggression is a function of the brain. The limbic system is the emotional part of the brain and if we have low serotonin in the limbic system, we have more aggressive behaviours. The frontal lobes are shaped by inborn temperament, but the environment (a parent who says, "No! We don't hit people!"), coupled with brain development, is responsible for suppression of the physical urge to hit, push, and bite. (Tremblay, 2005) Parents must address aggressive behaviour, not tolerate it.

Hitting and pushing also lessen as the child ages and the brain develops. As the brain grows, children learn to cope with emotions and develop more self-control. Children hit a lot when they are two (often once per day), less when they are five (perhaps once a week and usually siblings), and much less when they are eight (perhaps monthly). By school age, hitting may occur every few months. It usually happens more at home than at school. Most children stop hitting when they become teenagers. They learn to use their words instead. Then they discover the power of swear words! By age thirteen, when children can be charged with assault if they hit someone, most children will have learned more socially appropriate ways to manage their anger.

By age five, children learn about indirect aggression or passive aggressiveness as the result of their higher-order thinking skills. They can be sneakily aggressive in order to ensure they don't get caught, or get immediately hit back from the other child. This is a sign of brain development, as it takes higher-order thinking skills to weigh out the consequences in each act. By age five, children choose how to express anger. (Tremblay, 2005)

Small children take pleasure in hitting and slapping, as most adults do as evidenced when they spank in anger. It releases tension and feels satisfying for a second. However, we also realize that we are social groups and we can't be aggressive toward each other and still get along enough to live together. If we hit, we are sanctioned by the group: by isolation in the form of a time-out when we are young, by social ostracism during the school-age years, and finally, by jail as adults. Isolation is a big punishment for social mammals, whether humans or animals. Human isolation such as time-out teaches children not to do something, but doesn't offer instruction on what to do instead, like time-in does.

The key for parents is to keep repeating what you want them to do until they begin to take it on themselves. The more children practice calm-down tools, the more the tools are stored in their long term memory and come to mind as they internalize social and group rules. When children are exposed to social groups of all ages, in extended families and all-age schools, they learn the rules of controlling aggressive behaviour.

Societal disapproval helps children to suppress their anger acceleration. Young children are egocentric and don't care what others think about them. Their impulses rule their bodies and their brains. By school age, children are exposed to the wider world and care about what people think, so social isolation has a broader impact on their self-control. Nobody wants to be known as "The Hitter." Pride, shame, and embarrassment are effective social tools to keep mammals' aggression in check. (Tremblay, 2005)

Many parents worry that roughhousing and play fighting escalates into hurt feelings and real fighting. Play fighting does not encourage aggression. In fact, it is useful for development. Children discover their own limits and what other people consider acceptable, and this helps teach self-control. It's hard to watch as a parent, because you know one child is going to come to you crying, but it definitely teaches both children about boundaries. (Tremblay, 2005)

Environmental controls on aggression

Even if you are not the parent, as an adult you can play an important role in curbing children's aggression. Adults just need to do two things.

Do hold their hands and say, "Stop. No. Can you see this hurts your sister? Let's do this (stomp our feet on the floor) to express our anger." Children get to see their effect on others and can choose a nonviolent way to express their feelings. Repeat this message after every aggressive event.

Don't model hitting or any other aggressive behaviours. Children learn by modeling. Children who are hit are more likely to hit others by thinking that those who have power demonstrate it with physical aggression.

What about adults who can't control themselves? We all know people who demonstrate road rage, domestic abuse, or bar fights. What is going on for them? In research about murderers, it is found that these people have less-developed prefrontal cortexes. Although brain development is a function of nature and nurture, the environment has a big impact on the brain. Drugs, alcohol, and poor diet during pregnancy can affect the developing brain and impairs the ability to hit the brakes. Small children whose heads have been shaken show damage in this area, too. The prefrontal cortex gets banged against the skull. Thus, the brain area responsible for later planning, decision making, and executive function (the ability to cope with multiple demands) gets damaged. (Tremblay, 2005)

Poor language development and problem-solving abilities from lack of education, caring adults, and proper socialization, combined with weak emotional regulation, results in abnormal aggression in adults. It's a function of nature and nurture.

Most violent criminals have long histories of aggressive behaviour. They may have undiagnosed learning or behavioural disabilities. When they are disruptive in daycare or school, often they are sent to special programs, and later into delinquent centers that are not appropriate for their needs. Removing violent children from nonviolent kids hurts them. They don't learn proper behaviour and instead are lumped in with other aggressive people. (Tremblay, 2005)

Dominance without aggression is called leadership. It is worth investing the time and energy to show children how to use their brakes, as it gives them an edge in getting along with others for the rest of their lives.

It's sometimes two steps forward and one step back, but most children eventually learn how to handle anger in a way that doesn't hurt other people or damage other people's property. And it's usually during the teen years when this clearly and uniformly happens.

What makes our children angry?

- Unrealistic standards and expectations of them.
- Unmet needs; even babies get angry when hungry or not changed.

- Punishment and excessive competition and comparison to others.
- Sibling and peer conflict over issues.
- Feeling they have been treated unfairly.
- Feeling they don't have enough control and choices over their space, time, possessions, and lives.
- Goals are thwarted.
- Getting physically hurt.
- Having their treasures take away.

Typical ways children express their anger

Babies—red face, crying and grunts of protest.

Toddlers and preschoolers—hitting, pushing, biting, screaming, yelling, crying, tantrums, throwing things, flailing, and stomping feet. They may also hold their breath or vomit.

Middle childhood—teasing, bullying, sarcasm, hitting, yelling, crying, pinching, throwing, swearing, withdrawal, sulking and "attitude."

Adolescence—sulking, teasing, sarcasm, hitting, swearing, yelling, throwing, spitting, depression, withdrawal, and "attitude."

Many children do not "speak" about their anger, but "show" their anger. Children act out anger in direct ways such as biting, screaming, and tantrums and indirect ways such as sarcasm, attitude, and sadness. Children who feel their anger is unacceptable will act out in indirect ways. It takes a lot of practice for children to "use their words" rather than their bodies to express anger. They need to learn that anger that is expressed and accepted loses its destructive power, so it's always better to tackle anger directly than indirectly.

Reducing children's anger triggers

- Use solution-oriented, relationship-building discipline tools such as problem-solving.
- Avoid issuing logical consequences which can incite anger and rarely solves the problem. Problem-solve with your child instead.
- Have realistic expectations for your child's age and stage.
- Avoid hitting (hitting teaches hitting).
- Avoid isolating your child, such as using parent-controlled time-outs for her, if

it compounds her anger.

- Avoid comparing your children. Celebrate each child's uniqueness.
- Avoid experiences that are too hard for your child if she is frustrated easily.
- Actively listen to your child's frustration.
- Recognize when your child is having a cranky day and avoid too many demands on her during that time. Crankiness is just like being sick. It's an illness of the emotions and mind, not the body. Ease up on duties and let things slide. Tomorrow you can go back to the regular schedule when everyone is in a better mood.
- "Scold" the furniture or toy that was "causing trouble" for your child if they bang their body parts on it.
- Teach your child assertiveness language such as using I-statements.
- Accept and welcome your child's assertive language as above. The home is the best place for them to practice as long as it is respectful. Give their requests consideration to show them that I-statements really work.

Helping Children Manage Their Anger

Time-in is for them! They need a parent's help to calm down. The anger acronym works for children too.

A = Accept it

N = Neutralize the energy

G = Get away

E = Examine why

R = Return and problem-solve

A = Accept that children feel angry

Teach them to recognize anger and develop a vocabulary for naming their feelings. You can do this by:

- Sharing your feelings especially when you are angry.
- Encouraging your child to take ownership of feelings: "You felt mad…" instead of "He made you mad… " "It's okay to feel angry, but you can't hit your brother."
- Use angry people in stories, videos, and TV as a springboard for discussion. "It's normal for that girl to feel angry, but she probably shouldn't have thrown her

present in the garbage. Can you think of another way she could have expressed her anger? Should she have said, "I'm angry?"

N = Teach children how to neutralize their anger energy in a way that doesn't hurt anybody or wreck anything

Important note: the best time to teach this skill is not in the heat of the moment. Do it at a neutral time such as when out for a walk, at dinner, or even better, at bedtime tuck-in.

Use the same list of calm-down tools outlined for managing parents' anger (in the "**N**" section of Step 1). The same tools work for children, too. Here are some additional ones that work especially well for children.

- Make a poster of "yes" and "no" behaviours. We often tell children what they can't do, but not what they can do when we are in the heat of the moment. Write "yes" behaviours in green marker and "no" behaviours in red marker. Be sure there are more options on the green side! Discuss this when they are not angry.

- Make a feelings intensity poster. Draw a big "emotion" or "anger" thermometer on a poster and laminate it. When the child is angry, have her draw or color in red how much anger she feels. Have gradations from mild anger, such as "annoyed," to intense anger, such as "furious."

- Model healthy expressions of anger. Remember that kids learn how to deal with stress by watching their parents. Hitting, yelling, and throwing teaches our children to hit, yell, and throw.

- Repeat an inside joke, like, "Oops-a-daisy!" to put the humour back into the situation.

- Give your child a hug. Unless the child is mad at you, he might welcome hugs when he is angry.

- Offer a drink. Say, "Let's go and get your cup" to divert your child's energy.

- Give chewing gum to help calm down.

- Get your child to drink a glass of water through a straw. Sucking helps calm children.

- Get the current novelty stuffed animal. Say, "Let's bite the bird" or "Let's press the 'bird button.'"

- Gather a bunch of tin cans for your child to throw outside.

- Actively listen to your child's feelings. Say, "It's okay to cry and be angry."

- Extract yourself from your child's anger by saying, "I'm going to go and get you some water." or "I have to go use the washroom. I'll be right back."

- Give your child a batch of red Playdough® to pound.

- Act like you are angry, too. Calm people tend to escalate angry people.

- Say, "Grrrr! That is so annoying, isn't it?"

- Get a hanging bag, bean-bag chair, bouncy ball, or bop-it for your child to punch. Yes, it is very physical, but so are young children until they get better at verbalizing their anger. They express their feelings in body language and it is physical. It doesn't escalate their anger, but it does express the physical energy so they can be calmer. Don't worry, they won't always be hitting bop-it bags.

Some parents can't remember to actively listen or acknowledge their child's feelings when they think they should. It sometimes helps to make it your first response when reacting to anger. With practice, in time, it will just naturally happen.

G = Teach children to get away for while to think

Teaching children to temporarily walk away from a volatile situation is probably one of the best anger-management tools you can teach them. Teach them that the anger trigger is like a baited hook. They can choose to take it on and resolve it or leave it be and move on to other things. My daughter was 12 when she and her cousin were walking home from a store. They had a disagreement and both children were very angry. My daughter came home alone and I asked, "Where is your cousin?" My daughter replied, "We had a fight. I was so angry, I had to walk away." I explained to my daughter that her action was a good one, but in this circumstance, when her cousin was visiting from another city and didn't know where she was, it was not the best choice! We rushed into the car and found her cousin.

E = Help children examine the reasons why they feel angry

Actively listening to a child's anger and really trying to understand and empathize with his feelings helps him sort out the real underlying issues and primary feelings. Help him clarify why he is angry and what his primary feeling is. Is he jealous? Feeling victimized? Feeling tired?

Accept and validate all responses, even if the child is very angry with you. This is difficult to do but very helpful for the child. When your daughter says that she feels unloved compared to her sibling, the first words out of you are probably in defense: "But that's not true! You know I love you as much as her!" Active listening would elicit a response such as, "You feel unloved compared to your sister? You think that I love her more?" This shows your daughter that you have truly heard and validated her feelings and not dismissed them. Then you can defend. "I really love you just as much as your sister! How can I show you that?"

What is behind children's anger?

Children feel anger as the emotion behind the first emotion:

Fear—Your child fears a loss of the parent's love.

Tiredness—Your daughter had too many sleepovers and has a very short fuse.

Stress—Your children are overbooked with too many activities and not enough downtime.

Loss—Your child lost his favourite stuffed animal.

Jealousy—Your child thinks that you love the new baby more.

Hurt—Your child thinks you have time only for her sibling.

Embarrassment—Your daughter is yelled at in front of her friends.

Disappointment—Your daughter is not asked to the prom.

Hunger—Your child needs food to keep his blood sugar levels up.

You can use words to validate your child's feelings and help them calm down. The left column are words of parents' typical response and the right column is what to say instead:

Parent words that dismiss angry feelings	Active listening words to use to accept angry feelings
Stop making such a fuss.	I hear your anger.
Can't you be nice?	You sound pretty mad at that.
Good little girls don't act that way.	That's okay. Girls can feel angry just as much as boys.
It's not the end of the world.	You feel sad like it's the end of the world?
You don't really hate your baby brother.	You feel jealous of your baby brother?
In this house, we never say the word "hate."	Hate is a pretty strong word to adults. Is that the word you want to use?

Stop crying or I will give you something to cry about.	It's okay to cry. It helps us feel better.
You're ungrateful.	You are feeling victimized or treated unfairly?
What's wrong with you?	Something's wrong? Want to talk about it?
Don't be a baby!	It's okay to feel upset.
You're not really angry. You are just tired.	You seem pretty angry and tired also.
Why do you have to act that way?	You are feeling angry and frustrated?
Suck it up, Princess.	It's okay to feel angry.

Remember that actively listening to or acknowledging a child's strong emotions doesn't mean that you agree with them. It only means that you accept and validate what your child is feeling in the moment. It's their reality, no matter how rational or irrational it is. It conveys unconditional love and builds the relationship. The time for sorting out logic is after the emotions have cooled down.

R = Show children how to return to the person or situation and solve the problem directly

Surrender—Is it that big of a deal? Can the person be a bigger person and let it go? In our family, we have a "Bigger Person" badge that we made for the child to wear if they let the other sibling "win" for that time. Then the children would fight over who got to claim the badge!

Leave—Walking away and letting go is also a resolution and a valid choice.

Negotiate—Help children problem-solve and generate solutions if they require assistance. Teach trading, negotiation, taking turns, brainstorming options, and choosing solutions. For example, if one sibling wants what the other has, the rule may be that he has to find another item that would appeal to the sibling, so she is enticed to trade.

Teach them to first try to resolve the issue with other person involved before appealing to a higher authority.

Congratulate your child on small victories of self-control and demonstrated maturity. Learning to handle anger is a lifelong accomplishment.

Temper Tantrums

 "If we put as much time into helping our children handle their strong feelings as we do in keeping them in time-out, we would have emotionally healthy children." ~ Dr. Otto Weininger, Author

Temper tantrums are typical from ages one to four years or before the child is old enough to be sufficiently verbal to express his feelings. In spirited children, tantrums can last into the early school-age years.

In the new DSM-5, the Diagnostic and Statistical Manual of Mental Disorders, Fifth Edition, (American Psychiatric Association, 2013), tantrums are not considered a problem unless the child is older than six years and has at least three violent tantrums per week for at least six months duration. Most toddlers grow out of regular tantrums by age three to four years.

Tantrums occur when the child has a desire but can't understand her physical, mental, emotional, or social limitations. The child can't verbalize feelings of anger and frustration, tiredness, hunger, crankiness, or boredom, so she expresses feelings in body language by screaming, crying, kicking, or "doing the plank" (they flatten their arms over their heads and keep their bodies straight so a parent can't pick them up).

Tantrums are not planned, deliberate behaviour. They occur spontaneously in toddlers and preschoolers from an eruption of anger and frustration emotions and most children do grow out of tantrums naturally. Tantrums become an anger expression choice in school-aged and teen years. By that age, children can choose how to express their anger. If parents don't give in to tantrums, they will lessen.

Tantrums are not misbehaviour, nor are they abnormal or need correction. Children punished for temper tantrums learn to not express feelings. They learn how to suppress feelings, which is not healthy for the body or mind. Like an air mattress unable to express air through the main chute, it will spring leaks in other places to compensate. Most often, children will leak feelings through their "misbehaviour." Feelings must come out somewhere, somehow—even when parents are not comfortable with them.

There are two types of tantrums: "spill-over" and "power struggle."

Spill-over tantrums

Prevention: Food, rest, stimulation, or sleep when needed. Don't attempt shopping with a tired, cranky, or hungry child. Watch for and prevent triggers. Change the activity. As soon as you notice your child getting tired, hungry, or cranky, try a juice box (to increase her blood sugar) and a protein snack. Try cuddling her on your lap with a good book—a great way to calm down, learn literacy skills, and enjoy connecting quiet time together. Try and meet the child's needs as soon as possible as a tantrum is starting, if not before. Sometimes boredom can't be alleviated. Parents have to get creative and invent ways for children to pass the time.

Handling: Despite your best preventive techniques, tantrums will occur. You are not the only parent with a child that displays a tantrum in a public place. Other parents' children have done it before and will do it again. Those stares are not looks of judgment on your parenting ability. Other parents will look at you and breathe a sigh of relief that their children are normal, too. Go on about your activity as if nothing is happening. Sometimes ignoring it helps. Hold him if out in public, or move him to a safe quiet place. Let the child feel his feelings and know that expressing them is okay. Say, "That's okay. You're angry. I'll stay with you. Calm down." In a loud voice, so onlookers know that you have everything under control, say, "It's okay to be angry. I know you are feeling frustrated." Later, in a quiet moment, you could ask, "Do you want me to hold you for a minute while you calm down or would you rather be alone?" Your child's reaction will give you clues as to what he wants you to do. After the tantrum, carry on with your scheduled activity. Stay with your child. Use a soft, firm voice. Encourage deep breaths.

After: Wait for the calm after the storm. Avoid talking to your child during the storm because the child is too upset to hear anything. Again, try and meet her needs for rest and food as soon as possible. Label your child's emotions and give her the words to use so she develops a feeling vocabulary. Say, "Were you angry when you couldn't have that cookie while we were shopping?" The child usually understands the intent of the question and feels understood. It also gives her the words to match her uncomfortable feelings so she can "use her words" when she is older instead of her body language to express the feelings.

Power-struggle tantrums

Prevention: Offer lots of choices. Acknowledge your child's feelings of unhappiness. Pick your battles wisely.

Handling: Ignore the behaviour if your child is safe. Use a soft firm voice. Do not give in to your child's desire. Children do not do what doesn't work. If a tantrum always gets a prize, then it can become a conscious behaviour that will be repeated over and over as the child gets older. This is the hardest part of parenting with structure! Stay with your "No" and accept that the tantrum is coming. You will survive!

After: Wait for the calm after the storm. As with spill-over tantrums, acknowledge your child's feelings with an emotion word so he develops a feeling vocabulary. Carry on with your normal scheduled activity. When your child is calm, problem-solve the power struggle issue to prevent the misunderstanding from happening again. Talk about why the cookie was unacceptable and what your child could have in the store next time. Get his input.

General tips

Realize that tantrums are normal behaviour for young children. Don't be embarrassed. Every parent has been through them.

Older children are not immune to tantrums. Some children go through them sporadically into the school years. (Greene, 2010) See the book, *The Explosive Child* by Ross Greene, for more recommendations on school-aged tantrums.

Make the surroundings safe. If your child holds her breath and you are worried about cyanosis (lack of oxygen to her brain), blow gently into the child's face or apply a small splash of water on her to bring her out.

Avoid responding to your child's anger with anger. Stay calm. A parent's anger can escalate the intensity of the child's anger. When a child is out of control, the parent needs to be in control.

Try to prevent tantrums as much as possible with distraction. Get down on the floor and start to play with some of his toys. He will soon join you. Although preschoolers are more able to use their words, they can become overwhelmed with emotions and regress back to body language tantrums.

Avoid time-outs to deal with tantrums. Children are experiencing their feelings. Mostly, they don't understand them and can be overwhelmed with them. They don't yet have the self-control to contain their feelings. Some benefit with a parent time-in and some are okay with the parent just carrying on what she was doing.

Avoid punishing your child for having a tantrum. They are not a discipline issue. They are a brain-development, self-control issue that will resolve itself with age and maturity.

Children's uncontrollable anger can be frightening for them, especially for younger children. They need us to accept their feelings, love them with their feelings, and guide them through their outbursts with understanding, acceptance, and help. Parents can't do that if they shoo their children away during a time-out.

Many adults still need practice in controlling and managing their emotional temper tantrums. Eighty percent of people don't lose their jobs due to technical incompetence, but rather the inability to get along with other people and manage their anger and uncomfortable feelings in the workplace. (Armstrong, 1999)

As a society, we have a greater acceptance of positive emotions than negative ones, yet both kinds exist and are equally valid. In children, we find the positive ones don't quite bother us as much as the negative ones. At least they are easier on the ear! It's great that tantrums cease as children become more verbal and can express their feelings with words.

Self-control comes with brain development

Just as every child has an individual schedule for achieving toilet training or learning to read, so does every child have a schedule for achieving self-control and containing emotional expression. Some children are ahead of others and can control their actions sooner. Some are later.

Ninety-five percent of children grow into adults who can control their anger. I can't say this enough, because parents worry; children have at least thirteen years, from birth to teenage onset, to practice resolving their anger in ways that don't offend anyone. They can't complete this process by age two. Many parents look at the behaviour of a two-year-old and think, "I have to nip this anger thing in the bud right now or it will snowball. I will then have to deal with a fifteen-year-old who can't handle his anger other than tantrums and hitting! So I have to be very strict with this two-year-old!" This is not true! A fifteen-year-old is at a different stage and has much more brain development and self-control. Don't project ahead when you parent today. You will be a different parent and you will have a different child.

Anger must not be punished

We don't punish children who are in wheelchairs for not being able to climb stairs. We accept their physical limitations. We also should not punish young children who have emotional limitations. It is not their fault. Nor is it a sign of bad parenting. We can guide and teach children how to handle their emotions, and they will get better and better at it with time and development.

My son used to throw daily, almost hourly tantrums at the age of two. One day, when he was four, I was taking all five children and two friends swimming. I only had enough change in my pocket for one treat to share among all the children. I was bracing for the "after swimming-I'm so hungry" tantrum from my son, and after I explained the situation to him, he got it! No tantrum! I could actually negotiate with him. What a difference a year or two made in his frustration tolerance!

How to move a toddler having a tantrum

The best way to carry a toddler who is having a tantrum is face out with one of your arms between her legs, and grasping your other arm around her trunk and under both of her arms. You can also hold the handle of a baby carrier or shopping bags on your arm, if you find yourself in the middle of a store with a baby and a toddler having a tantrum. It helps to bring someone along if you know that your child is prone to tantrums in stores, just to help with packages, kicked-off shoes, and to provide an extra set of hands.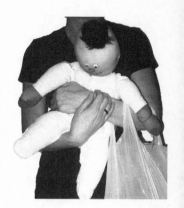

It's also helpful to schedule shopping without the child if store tantrums are a huge problem. The child will grow out of it, but for now, it's the easiest thing to do. You also might wish to avoid problem areas like malls where it's hard to get to a car quickly or stores that are especially difficult, like candy and toy shops. Shop alone and have a partner or babysitter home with the children. This stage will only last a few months.

How to get a toddler into a car seat during a tantrum

Throw your packages into the driver's seat. Gently, but firmly, place the child in the car seat. She may be doing "the plank," so it might help to tickle her to get her to bend and put the bar down to strap her in. Let her have a tantrum, and you could gently stroke her hair or hand while she finishes. Show her how to breathe deeply. Softly talk to her. "It's okay." "Let's breathe." If the noise is too much, close the door and wait outside so she can see you and feel assured that you won't leave her. Stay calm!

Celebrate your toddler's "No!"

I walked into the kitchen and discovered my two-year-old, blonde-haired daughter, Heidi, dressed in her little pink fleece sleeper with the padded feet, standing on top of the chair next to the counter. She was preoccupied with dipping her fingers into the butter bowl and then into the sugar bowl before they headed into her waiting mouth. When she saw me enter the kitchen, a potential threat to her wonderful activity, she formed a very concise pointed finger at me and firmly delivered "No!" at my astonished expression.

"No!" It's probably the most commonly used word in toddlerhood! It flies out of our children's mouths before they even have time to really think about what they are saying "no" to.

When my five children were young, they were allowed to say "no" as much as they wanted to. I would always try to respect their "no" as much as I could within the parameters of the particular situation, and especially in circumstances such as when they didn't want to be tickled by me, or didn't want to hear me sing, or didn't want to be kissed by Grandma or didn't want to share their prized possessions. I think "no" is an important word for children to practice asserting their feelings and desires, and unless it is a matter of safety, they have the right to have their opinion listened to and respected. Here is why children should be allowed to say "no":

- I want my daughter to say "no" when she is three and her daddy might want to put her in the front seat and not the car seat because it is less of a hassle.

- I want my son to say "no" when he is five and his little five-year-old friend might want him to cross a busy street without an adult.

- I want my daughter to say "no" when she is nine and her uncle might want to touch her in her private places.

- I want my son to say "no" when he is twelve and his friends might want him to steal a candy bar from the grocery store.

- I want my daughter to say "no" when she is fourteen and her friends might bully a fellow student.

- I want my son to say "no" when he is fifteen and a friend's drunk parent might want to drive him home from a party.

- I want my daughter to say "no" when she is sixteen and her boyfriend might not wish to respect her boundaries.

- I want my son to say "no" when he is eighteen and his buddies might want him to try some "ecstasy."

So when she is two-years-old, my daughter can practice saying "no" as much as she needs to. And I won't take it personally.

Spirited children's tantrums

Spirited children don't handle frustration very well. They may have more tantrums than an easy-going child; their tantrums may be hourly or daily. Brandie, a mom in a parenting group, said, "I have a very spirited three-year-old who does the *opposite* of any requests." Three to five-year-olds are into power, and it's totally developmentally appropriate and the spirited temperament trait gives that power the persistence that makes parenting challenging. Head off the triggers as best as you can for spill-over tantrums, and never, ever, ever give in to the power struggle ones. It really increases the likelihood of them doing it again.

On the other hand, Donna, another mom, experienced the three-and-a-half-year-old solution! It seemed that three-and-a-half was the magic age that spirited children changed. Temper tantrums normally dissipate after children reach three-and-a-half years old. They can go from daily tantrums to once-a-month tantrums almost overnight at that age. Children really turn a milestone as they become much more cooperative, remember things, and negotiate better. Many moms of spirited children have reported the same thing.

I have found that heading off the triggers helps for spirited children. Then, if you gradually increase the triggers or expose children to frustrating incidents more as they get older, they get practice at learning to handle their strong feelings better. The frequency of times they feel frustrated or angry naturally increases as they get older, by natural consequences. Sometimes, you just can't hold a tantrum off. That broken banana just can't be fixed, and it has to be *that* banana! Tell them, "It's okay to feel that way." Help them with their strong emotions when you say "no." Try to hold them (but don't force it if they refuse), speak softly with, "That's okay. You can feel angry," and try to rock them, rub their back, or rub their hand until the tantrum is over. It tells them that all their feelings are acceptable and you love them unconditionally—that the tantrum has a start and a finish. It also tells them you will not back down and say "yes" if you are engaged in a power struggle.

It's very difficult to remain calm and unfettered through it, but try! Protect yourself and anyone else. Hold the child's hands while speaking softly if she is prone to hit or throw during a tantrum. Save your words for later, when she can hear you better.

Remember, this too shall pass! Even spirited children gain more self-control, but it may not be at four or five, but later at seven or eight years of age.

Steps that parents can take to avoid public scenes of anger

Have realistic expectations. Toddlers won't sit in a restaurant chair for more than ten minutes, in spite of how much we need them to. Proper table and social manners can be taught much later, when the child is older and can understand respect for other's needs. Age five is a good time to start teaching table manners. As well, parents know their child's temperament and their limits best. Some children are naturally quieter than others and can sit still for an hour in their highchair while amusing themselves; others won't sit still for five minutes. It's not the child's fault for these differences in self-control. It's how they are. By age ten most children will sit still and have reasonable table manners!

Break errands up into smaller trips. A three-to-four-hour shopping trip may be too much stimulation for a toddler or preschooler to handle.

Before going out in public, try to have a rested and fed child. Adults get cranky when they are hungry and tired, and children are no different. Shopping for groceries before afternoon naptime may be too taxing for a toddler. When the preschooler gives up naps, he still has a cranky time of day when he used to nap. This is not a good time to shop. Bring along juice boxes and keep non-perishable snacks in the car for unexpected delays in the car or long lines in stores.

Distraction is a great tool for children this age who experience boredom quite quickly. A snack works while waiting for dinner in restaurants or in stores. Bring along a special "going out" toy bag that you bring out only in public. In long lines, children can play with a container of Playdough®, a calculator, a pull toy, or a roll of tape. Older children can play card games or "I-spy" with you, or play "Rock-paper-scissors." Children's books are a handy way to pass the time waiting in offices and stores. It's a great way to build literacy in everyday life and spend some one-on-one time.

Language builds emotional competence. Parents are best able to boost their child's language by naming objects, but can do it just as well naming feelings and emotions. When children can express their anger in words, they gain a valuable life skill.

Distractions such as phones and tablets are not the best idea. Often, children throw them when they are angry because they have to give them back to the parent. Current research shows that the more children spend in front of screens, the less language skills they have. (Fowler, 2013) We are currently raising the "silent" generation by our reliance on screens as babysitters and pacifiers.

As well, children who learn in three dimensions with physical items, such as books and Playdough®, do better academically than with two-dimensional items such as screens.

The human parent-child interaction, which is called the "serve and return response," stimulates young children's brains far better than screens; so next time, pick up a book and read it to your child, instead of parking her in front of your phone or tablet.

You don't have to rely on cell-phone applications, portable handheld gaming devices or media players and other electronic devices to occupy your kids during waiting times. The constructive ideas below will stimulate imagination, creativity, intellect, problem-solving and social skills. Best of all, they don't require cables or batteries, can be taken anywhere, and will amuse toddlers to teens.

All of these items should fit in a small 9 x 12-inch container, such as a rectangular plastic box with a snap lid, a lunch bag, a backpack, or even a laptop side pocket or briefcase for ease of carrying to restaurants, doctors' offices or airports.

The busy brain distraction kit for all ages

1. **Pipe cleaners**—These versatile little wires can be molded into cars, people, and many other items for make-believe play.

2. **Playdough®**—Keep it moist in a plastic bag. Kids can make 3D sculptures for toys. With a digital camera, teens can make animated figure movies.

3. **Masking tape or cellotape**

4. **Scissors**—Make sure it's safety scissors for younger children.

5. **Small whiteboard**—and dry-erase markers, with a cloth for erasing. Endless opportunities to make signs, keep game scores, or play picture games.

6. **Colouring markers**—My kids used to colour the doctor's waiting room bed-covering paper!

7. **Pens and pencils**—Play hangman or other words games. Write in a journal or just draw!

8. **Plain paper**—for drawing houses and scenes, or constructing cars, buildings, items and people, to be coloured, cut out, and assembled with tape and scissors.

9. **Deck of cards**—Great for teens to play Cheat, Snap, Spoons, Rummy, Blackjack, Uno, and many other games. Rules can be found on the internet.

10. **Dice**—for playing addition, multiplication, and chance challenges. Dice also work with homemade board games created from the above items.

The play value in this box of items will last a long time, especially if you only keep it for on-the-go errands. Encourage your school-ager or teen to bring along a book, too.

Engage your child to help. Toddlers can put apples into bags at grocery stores or carry a special brand of juice to the cart. They can even put some of your hand-picked groceries into those cute little child-sized carts at the supermarket. Just watch your ankles! Offer them a choice between two acceptable products so they feel they are really helping you. My toddler learned about counting, shapes, and colors while grocery shopping because I constantly talked to him in the cart. I named items. We played lots of peek-a-boo and "I spy" games during waiting times. This was much more fun, interactive, and brain-building than giving him an app on a device.

Take into account children's high energy needs. When you are going somewhere where children are expected to be quiet, make sure your toddler has burned off some energy beforehand. Visit a playground before the wedding or church service or a meeting. If traveling on a bus or plane, bring a ball along to chase between travel times. Children need to expend energy every hour. It's no use getting angry at children for being "rambunctious" when they are just being children.

Handling public tantrums

My very spirited daughter was two when she threw a tantrum on a plane. She wanted to get down from my lap, and the flight attendants wanted her to sit still during take-off. Take-off was delayed, and the tantrum lasted at least thirty minutes. She was screaming, crying, hitting, and flailing. It was a captive show, with 238 other people watching my parenting skills! We got through it.

When she was fourteen and flying with me to Australia on a trip that took five plane rides and forty-eight hours non-stop with a meager few hours of sleep, she was the strong, stoic one to console me, her mother. I was bone tired and threw a tantrum when the flight attendant woke me up to ask me to move my seat forward so the people behind me could eat another meal. I lost it and cried uncontrollably. My daughter was very comforting as she put her arms around me and softly said, "It's okay, Mom. You're tired and it's okay."

When she was twenty and accompanied me to Paris, we went up to all the parents on the plane that were struggling with screaming toddlers and assured them not to worry and said "This too shall pass!" My daughter just smiled.

Despite the best of intentions in avoiding public scenes or trying to prevent them, a tantrum may occur. Sometimes a parent has to run an errand at the wrong time or forgot to pack a toy or snack, and the child emotionally explodes. What can a parent do? Take a deep breath and remain calm. You are the adult. So you are expected to be calm, even when embarrassment and subsequent anger are rising up in your throat. Our job as parents is to teach self-control. The best way is to model it. Get yourself calm, then get your child calm, and then solve the problem. Calmly pick him up and take him out to the car, restroom, or a quiet place to wait out the tantrum.

How do you cope with people's stares? Ignoring helps. We may feel that other people are judging us. Some might be, but others may be silently empathizing and remembering their own days of dealing with toddlers. Often they really do understand but don't know what to say or do to help you. Have confidence in your parenting. Say in a really loud voice, "It's okay, Sophia. I'm here," while you wait until the tantrum is over. Or, "It's okay, we are going to leave now." People know that you are calm and in control, or at least look that way! Take a deep breath. Avoid threatening your child and raising your voice. Avoid threatening to leave the child. You never would anyway, and it destroys trust and attachment between parent and child. Anger tends to escalate anger. One of you has to remain calm, and it isn't likely to be your toddler.

If someone makes a rude comment, you can politely say, "I am taking care of the situation," and carry on doing what you plan to do. You know your child best and can advocate for them. Many well-meaning friends, family, and strangers, especially those that say, "All that child needs is a good spanking," may not know the needs and developmental capabilities of young children or they forget what it is like to have to constantly meet those needs. Let it go.

When we see other parents coping with a toddler's tantrum, it may be nice to offer them some words of encouragement. A simple "It's hard when toddlers have tantrums. You deserve a nice cup of tea!" or "It's tough parenting. Is there anything I can help with?" Often moms need a hand to carry the baby, push a stroller, or handle packages while they carry their screaming child to the car. A smile can even go a long way to alleviate a parent's embarrassment and often helps calm both the parent and the child. When my daughter was having the airplane tantrum, the flight attendant patted my shoulder and said, "You're doing fine." I felt instantly better and less anxious. My daughter probably picked up on my feelings and felt better, too.

Dealing with angry preschoolers and young school-aged children

- Actively listen and hold the angry child if she consents. Rub her back. Put her hand in both of yours and gently rub.

- Teach self-calming tools in a calmer time and remind him in the turmoil time.

- Be a "feeling releaser" listener rather than a "fact finder" listener, especially when dealing with fighting children who are very angry at each other.

- Acknowledge your child's anger and assure her you are available to help.
- If your child is breaking something, stop him! Direct him to a tool from the calm-down list. When my son was seven and totally frustrated that he couldn't beat Bowser® in Mario 64®, he threw down his controller and repeatedly jumped on his black N64® console. When I saw what he was doing, I grabbed him off of it and directed him to the sofa where he could punch the cushions. I had to stay with him to ensure he wasn't going to wreck anything else. This was a better target to release the energy. Remember that for younger children, physical anger expression that doesn't hurt anybody or anything is appropriate.

When the child is angry at you

Stay calm, even if the anger is directed at you. Breathe deeply. Visualize calm. Don't react. Fake it until you make it! You can choose to stay calm.

If you can do it, use the active listening tool: say, "I can see that you are angry at me because I said 'No.'" Then leave it at that. Don't provide explanations or justifications, even if they are very valid. Now is not the time to teach. Now is the time to help her get calm. You can teach, rationalize, and justify after she is calm.

You are not the target - Don't take anger personally

Older school-aged children's anger

Twelve-year-old Jackson didn't like his mom's answer to his request for a sleepover that night. She was tired and didn't feel up to monitoring a "wakeover"—really, do they ever sleep? Jackson thought that his mom was being unreasonable. When she maintained her "No" after several pleas, Jackson couldn't contain his anger at her. He kicked the garbage can and spilled the contents all over the kitchen, pushed his little brother's backpack out of the way of his coat (knocking papers out of the backpack), grabbed his coat and slithered into his shoes while walking out the door and slamming it. He walked three blocks to the store to get an iced drink and get a grip.

Meanwhile, Jackson's mom was also angry. Shouldn't kids accept parental authority without getting angry all the time? As a fervent advocate of parenting completely without punishment, this is a common question I get from parents in my classes. How do parents handle this type of scenario without punishing or escalating the child's anger or their own?

The first thing to keep in mind is that children have the right to feel angry. It's part of the palette of human emotions. Everyone feels angry during various moments and it's a normal, useful emotion. Anger is a part of our biological makeup, as much as our feet, chins, and elbows. We must accept that our children are not going to like us, our opinions, or our actions from time to time and that is perfectly okay. It's their job to accept our limits, and it's our job to stay with our "no."

Second, we must teach our children not to limit their anger and feelings, but only how to limit the expression of them. Jackson's feelings of anger was okay. Kicking the garbage can, shoving the backpack, and slamming the door was not okay. Grabbing his coat and going for the walk was great. Swearing and grumbling was not.

Third, as parents in the line of fire, we often feel angry when our children are angry at us. That's okay, too. We are allowed to feel angry. However, we often get carried away and meet expressions of their anger with expressions of our own anger: when we get yelled at, swore at, hit, or otherwise abused, we threaten ultimatums, issue consequences, spank, yell, or force our children into a time-out. We react. None of that is helpful. The problem is that it's punitive and only serves to escalate everyone's anger. It also damages our valuable parent-child bond. We can feel angry, but the best way to deal with our anger is to take a parent time-out. Being sworn at and hit as parents is not right and definitely needs to be addressed, but the timing and manner of handling it are important.

Handling children's anger in a way that builds your bond

1. Stay calm. Deal with your own rising anger by taking a time-out physically, emotionally, or cognitively. For your own self-preservation, get away from the other person's tirade. Go watch a video in another room. Pretend to read a book. Put in the iPod ear buds. Removing yourself from the scene defuses the situation. Ignore it if things are being broken by your school-aged child or teen. Now is not the time to deal with it. They will clean it up later when they are calm.

2. For young children, try to distract them with a movie or new activity. They often need help calming down and isolation time-outs escalate their anger and often erupt into power struggles. Never force a time-out. Offer to sit with them someplace more calming. Take them out of the vortex of anger by carrying them to a calm, quiet space. Speak calm words or hum. Rock them in your lap to get them calm. Breathe with them. If they are trying to throw or break something, you are bigger than they are and can move them to a safer place. Just stay calm and wait until they get calm.

3. Make a mental note next time to pack away anything valuable until your child expresses their anger less destructively.

4. Don't clean or fix anything in the heat of the moment. Jackson's mom left the garbage mess and her other son's backpack mess for Jackson to face when he returned from the store in a calmer mood. As scary as it is for parents to witness the angry rampage and mess that children can make, it's important to show them that you are calm (even if you aren't on the inside!), you are the adult in control, and the mess they are making is not bothering you. The more they see that breaking things affects you, the more they will do it to punish you when they are angry. School-aged children "try out" behaviours to see the effect on you (now that they can understand consequences). If they see that it doesn't bother you, they won't break things again.

5. When everyone is calm, invite a talk. Express your concerns and listen without judgment to their point of view. Problem-solve for win-win solutions. Also brainstorm non-destructive ways to handle their anger for the next time.

6. Contract with them for a time that the result of their anger episode will be cleaned up, fixed, or restored to the satisfaction of all that it affects. Ensure that the school-aged or teenaged child does the work. Do not do this yourself! For younger children, like preschoolers and toddlers, you will have to help them. It is important to follow through on this. Do not take this step in the heat of the moment. It will escalate the power struggle.

7. Hug. Show your child that you love her and all her emotions unconditionally!

8. Model healthy ways to express anger yourself. Examine closely if you hurt others or things in the middle of expressing your anger.

Remember that learning to handle anger is a childhood process and even many adults struggle with it. Talk to other parents and you will see that they have problems containing their anger in parenting. Young children hit, bite, push, and throw things until they get more verbal. School-aged children sometimes hit, but more often throw things, slam doors, swear, and talk back. Teens swear, break, throw, and slam and yell. Adults hopefully use I-statements and parent time-outs! Ideally, all adults express anger well, but we know many that don't! They still revert back to childhood expressions such as door slamming, temper tantrums and throwing things.

Also, recognize that the less you punish your children, the stronger your bond becomes and they are more willingly to please you, and engage in their mess clean-up. Instead of punishing children, problem-solve and actively listen, as you do in all your other respectful relationships. Children, like adults, feel less angry when they have more input into decisions and situations that affect them.

Above all, embrace anger. It's a gift. Your children feel safe enough around you to express their honest feelings, even if it is not the most appropriate expression.

Handling teen-age anger and disrespect with calmness

Once, a dad found an angry rant directed at him on his teenage daughter's social media page. The dad was angry, and rightly so. He reacted by filming himself calmly wrecking her beloved laptop. He proceeded to upload it to the internet where it went viral.

Both dad and daughter were angry. In many ways, neither dad nor daughter was respectful toward the other. Good parenting involves mutual respect in a loving relationship. Mutual respect is treating another human being as no less and no more than one would like to be treated. Respect transcends age, race, religion, culture, and social status in importance in starting and maintaining relationships. Good parenting also involves addressing disrespectful behaviour in a respectful way.

Here are some "don'ts" and "dos" I have learned over my twenty-four years of parenting. They obviously work, because in the process of raising two teens and three adult children, I have never had a door slam in my house yet!

- Don't call your child names or put down her ideas.
- Don't talk about him disapprovingly in front of other people.
- Don't make faces at your children, roll your eyes, mimic them, or use words dripping with sarcasm.
- You are the leader and model for respectful behaviour. As the adult, you must rise above immature responses.
- Don't use your child's possessions, break them, or give them away without your child's permission.
- Don't go into your child's room, computer, drawers or closets to snoop. Don't allow the child's siblings or others to snoop either.
- Don't use sarcasm when addressing your child's behaviour, such as, "I'm not your slave. Make your own lunch!"
- Don't punish your child, which includes everything from grounding, time-out, and withdrawal of privileges to hitting, fines, and confiscating treasures.
- Don't yell, threaten, criticize, belittle, or punish your children in public, especially in front of their peers.
- Don't tell them to "suck it up," or "be a big boy," if they display feelings that you don't like.
- Don't call in the forces and go into full-frontal war mode when your child is disrespectful to you. Don't engage in a power struggle and fight (punish) any

way you can until you win. You may win the argument but you'll lose your connection, communication, sharing, and collaboration in the relationship.

- Don't turn away and let it go when your children are disrespectful. Call them on it by clearly explaining your expectations that everyone is treated with respect (and be sure you are modeling the same). Insist on restitution, apology, fixing the situation to make it better, or any steps you both think might help toward mending that relationship. When both of you are calmer, request a commitment from your child that he will work toward change. Set a time to talk.

- Don't ignore other people's children when they are disrespectful to you or others in public. As Hillary Clinton once said, "It takes a village to raise a child." Confront the child, and perhaps their parent if there is no change, and insist on civility and politeness.

- Do stay calm as much as you are able to. You need a calm frame of mind to deal with your child. Tell your child you are very angry and are going to take a short break if you need a few minutes to calm down.

- Do confront with your I-statement. ("I feel unappreciated when I upgrade your computer and you don't express thanks for my time and cost.")

- Do listen carefully to your child's response and be truly open to what she is feeling. Listening and validating her feelings doesn't mean you have to agree with them. ("You seem to feel upset about the amount of chores you have to do around the house.")

- Do problem-solve the situation. ("Let's go for a 'walk and talk' and see if we can find a solution that meets both our needs.")

- Do say "Please," "Thank you," and "I appreciate" to your child.

- Do apologize when you make a parenting blunder.

- Do look at backtalk as an opportunity to teach your child assertiveness with appropriate language skills.

- Do treat others, especially people in service roles, with politeness and kindness when your children are watching.

- Do treat your parenting partner with the same respect that you want. Don't use name-calling, put-downs, and sarcasm in your words. Do treat his treasures and accomplishments as items valuable and cherished.

In other words, promote respect, be a model of kindness and politeness and address learning situations respectfully with your children by problem-solving and using that old standby, listening!

"Attitude" is disguised anger

Attitude or sass is sarcastic anger. It is often a You-statement. What is your child really saying? She is trying to communicate even though it is in a poor form. If you look underneath, often it's a sign that your child is ready for more independence and feels thwarted in some way. Does she have reasonable choices? Can you give her more ability to make decisions? Or does she feel that she never has control over anything? Children want their needs and wants taken care of, just like adults do.

Once, my son, who was sixteen, was angry because he was struggling with a video game and I had asked him to do some chores. He replied with a "f#%K" word and kicked down the chair that was beside him. My anger rose and I said to him, "I'm angry and taking a time-out to calm down." I left and became calm. I didn't nag him to pick up the chair. That was not the time. He finished his game and left the room in a torrent of frustration. I'm not sure what he did to calm down, but I caught up with him about thirty minutes later. He was calm, I was calm, and we needed to solve the problem. I told him that I appreciated that he was angry, but I didn't like that word yelled at me. I suggested that he pick up the chair. He apologized and picked up the chair. My stern reaction was enough to let him know that he had offended me and could damage our relationship that was, on the whole, pretty good. He never directed a swear word to me again.

When looking at sass from your child, try to identify what they are really trying to communicate based on their needs or feelings (NOF), stripped of the sarcasm, and then rephrase it back to them. "You are upset because I'm interrupting your game?" Share your feelings. "When I hear your tone, I feel disrespected. I would like to talk about this. Can we try this again? Here is how you can say what you are feeling. Instead of saying, 'Whatever!' say 'I'm feeling nagged. Please leave me alone.' Then I will really hear you. Can you try that please?" Sometimes, you really have to give them the exact words to use, or they don't know the respectful way to assert their needs. It's a critical life skill to speak up respectfully so people can know what's bothering you but still not feel attacked. Or you could gently say, "Do you want a moment to rephrase that?" You could use humor in your response. You could also just walk away and your body language will reveal you don't want to be spoken to that way. Responding with anger or sarcasm doesn't teach them anything other than that it's okay for them to continue that way.

Be sure to model assertive politeness instead of "attitude". It's a hard trap not to fall into especially when family sarcasm is portrayed all over the media as cool and witty. It's a false representation. If you said, "whatever" to your boss when she asked you why your project was late, I would bet she wouldn't laugh. You are the perfect person to teach your children the assertiveness skills they need in life. Start at home!

On the left column are typical attitude statements. On the right are phrases you might want to teach your child to say instead of their attitude.

Attitude statements your child might use	Persuasive statements that adults listen to
You're not my boss!	I'd like a choice.
I hate you!	I didn't like what you said.
I'm not your slave.	That doesn't seem fair.
I'll do what I want.	I need to try.
You don't love me.	I need attention.
You don't understand.	Please listen to my opinion.
It's not fair.	I feel capable and responsible.
This is dumb.	I feel scared, worried, about failing.
I can't do it.	I don't know how.
I have rights!	Please help me.
Fine!	Please let me have a choice.
Whatever!	I'm feeling pushed.
I don't care.	I'm scared.

We must not be afraid of our children's anger

Even if you are afraid of your child's anger, don't let her see it. Children need to see you in control. Don't freak out! Fake calmness until it becomes real. If your teenager is wrecking her room, remember, it is her room! She will deal with it later, not you. Later, after the emotional temperature has gone down, help the child see the problem and generate some options for a solution.

My daughter was ten when I was driving her to a lesson. She asked for a sleepover that evening, which I wasn't up for. I said, "No." She was angry. During the entire 30 minute drive, she constantly kicked my little bag of garbage that I had hung on the armrests of the van's front seats. With each kick, garbage fell out. I was getting madder and madder. I couldn't stand it anymore, and pulled over to a hamburger restaurant. I had to break what was happening, as it was escalating. I parked the car and said to her, "I'm going to get a burger and calm down. I'm very angry right now. You can sit here or come in." After removing myself from her anger, she didn't have anyone to release it in front of and decided to come in. I ordered her a burger and we both ate in silence. I asked her to tell me in words that she was angry. I even gave her the words and asked her to say them. "I feel mad when you won't let me have a sleepover because I don't think it is fair." This was an I-statement that was respectful and revealed her true feelings. Then I acknowledged her feelings and said that it was okay to feel angry. Perhaps we could problem-solve the sleepover issue and find a solution that worked for both of us. We ended up agreeing to do it the next night. After we found a solution, she agreed to clean up the garbage in the van.

Once, when my daughter was 17, she rolled her eyes at me when I made a request. It was such a rare event, that I asked her, "What was that?" She replied, "Mom, that's my EYE-statement!"

Angry people want and need comfort

If you have a sulking teenager or stomping-up-to-the-room school-ager, recognize that people who are angry want their loved ones to care and notice. If you ignore their anger, they are going to escalate ways to express it so that you will notice. Teenagers who cut themselves or stuff their feelings with food want an adult to notice them and listen to their feelings.

For younger children, a hug and kinds words show them they are loved and that people care they are angry.

Give an older child some time and space to get calm. Then offer hugs while saying kind words. Acknowledge their anger. Then offer to help with problem-solving. After the situation is resolved, help or remind them to clean up whatever damage they have done in the middle of their anger. Did they throw something, kick something, break or damage something? Help them repair or replace it. Be sure they are the main workers and payers. If they have to face the results of their anger, they will be much more selective in how to express their anger next time.

Remember, no one older than a preschooler really "loses it." When we are older than seven, we make conscious decisions on how to express and neutralize our anger. When children clean up their anger mess, they learn to make better choices next time.

About Apologies

"Holding on to anger is like grasping a hot coal with the intent of throwing it at someone else; you are the one who gets burned."
~Gautama Buddha, Spiritual Teacher

When a child needs to apologize to someone else—nudge, don't force! Apologies must be sincere and they come when the apologizer is calm and ready to do it.

This is one sticky area in discipline. My son Scott was three and a half years-old and we were at the local science center. He was playing with the sticks and threw one at his brother. The stick went flying and almost hit another mom who was sitting down. Fortunately, it hit the wall. I grabbed Scott and insisted he apologize. Of course, he wouldn't. By that time he was feeling like he was on stage and embarrassed and shy. I temporarily let it go. We went to a new activity, and he calmed down. So did I. We talked about our feelings and reconnected. I then suggested it would be the right thing to do to go back and apologize. I didn't force it. I forgot about it and went back to talking to my friend. I noticed five minutes later that Scott went up to the mom and said he was sorry—on his own terms, in his own time, and in his own words and way.

Apologies must come from the heart. They almost never come when forced or in the emotional heat of the moment. They can be taught by modeling, not forcing the words. Parents never apologize in the heat of the moment. Why do we make children? Because it's more about our social embarrassment and need for social bandages than about how the child is feeling at the moment.

When your child hits another, the time to insist on an apology is not while he is still mad! Instead, shower the victim with attention and mend his wounds. Say, "We are really sorry for your hurt," so you are modeling an apology for your child. You are expressing sorrow for the victim. It doesn't excuse what the hitter did. It shows empathy from you. When the two children have cooled, you could remind your child that an apology is still on order. Nudge, teach, offer advice, but don't force!

It can be difficult to handle the parents of the other child, who may expect an apology from your child. It's best to be direct and say to the other parent, "Emma is too upset right now to apologize, but we will still deal with this." Or, "We will make this a teaching moment." It lets the other parent know that you are conscious of the social rules and are teaching your child about amends. It doesn't say you will force an apology and it still respects your child's need to apologize in her own time and method. You could also apologize yourself to the parents for your child's behaviour.

It shows them that you know the social rules and care about their feelings, and it's great modeling.

When the child needs to apologize to you

Tell the child you need to hear an apology to get past your hurt. This puts the focus of change on you and your needs rather than something he must do. Again, nudged apologies come faster than forced ones.

When you need to apologize to the child

Do it when it needs to be done! Be sincere. It doesn't undermine your parental authority or respect. If anything, children have more respect because it takes a big leap to admit wrong and make restitution for it. It helps to calm a child's anger and resentment if they have been treated unfairly. It's great modeling for the children in teaching how to do it sincerely and with respect. Apologies are essential in love relationships and that includes the parent-child one too.

Remember that even after the apology is issued, people need time to heal. Forgiveness comes when the other person is ready. Give them time and space and usually they will come around. If you are the person angry and the other person has sincerely apologized and feels remorse, don't hold a grudge. Let it go.

Temperament

Children are born with a distinct temperament and keep it throughout their life. About 40% of children are born "easygoing," about 30% are "slow-to-warm" and about 15 to 20% are born with a "spirited" temperament. There are eight temperament characteristics that represent a continuum of personality. They are: Adaptability, Persistence, Intensity, First Reaction, Mood, Regularity, Activity Level, and Sensitivity. When a child has five or more strong characteristics, they can be considered to have a more easy-going or spirited temperament. Both present unique challenges for parents, but it is important to remember that all children are different and may require a different response in various situations. All temperaments do well with a nurturing, but structured and non-punitive parenting style. (Sheedy Kurcinka, 2006)

Due to the persistence, intensity and difficulty in adapting, spirited children may have more opportunities to learn how to handle their anger and frustration. The benefit is that they have had lots of practice when they grow to be adults and are able to forge onward through life's difficulties.

Below is a chart to briefly outline the different challenges that all temperaments may face in childhood. These were generated from parents' observations of their children who came to my classes. When parents are sensitive to their children's temperament, they will adjust their parenting practices to support and encourage their children in managing their lifelong challenges.

Many parents report difficulty in parenting spirited children because conventional parenting techniques do not seem to work for spirited children. Spirited children were more resistive to parental authority and persistent in pressing for their own way. It was like parenting teens when the children were only two. Parents had to re-adjust their directives and philosophy of parenting because spirited children need more of everything; more planning, consideration, flexibility, patience, discussion and especially protection from criticism of others. With sensitive, nurturing and non-punitive structured parenting, they grow into very wonderful people.

For more information on specific parenting tips, see the books, *Raising Your Spirited Child*, by Mary Sheedy Kurcinka, and *Parenting The Fussy Baby and High-Need Child*, by Dr. William Sears and Martha Sears. In raising three spirited children, one easy-going child, and one slow-to-warm child, I found both books to be very helpful and provided the framework for the non-punitive tips in my book, *Discipline Without Distress*.

Benefits and challenges of eight temperament characteristics

Characteristic	Challenges	Benefits
Low Adaptability **Spirited** Temperament	These children challenge new rules and the status quo. They can be perceived as "trouble-makers." Change is very hard. Life changes such as moves or travel are very traumatic. Their growth could be limited because they pass on valuable experiences.	These children are certainly not wishy-washy! They have standards for acceptance of new ideas and situations and we always know where they stand. They are status-quo rule followers and are dependable, loyal, and consistent.

Characteristic	Challenges	Benefits
High Adaptability **Easygoing** Temperament	The child can be unfocused and scattered at times. He adapts easily to anyone and can go off with strangers. Can lose his sense of self.	The child will easily accept new rules. He travels well and is eager to try new things. Seizes opportunities. He will have less stress adjusting to life's curveballs.
Steadfast Persistence **Spirited** Temperament	These children need patience and could be too driven. They may be perceived as stubborn; it's hard for them to know when to "let go" for health reasons. Can be perceived as demanding, irritating, and wearing. Their persistence is stressful to themselves and others, as they don't know when to quit.	These children tend to be accomplished and very motivated. They have determination and many become leaders and entrepreneurs. They are very productive in whatever they do. They get what they want and are often very successful in attainment of goals.
Low Persistence **Easygoing** Temperament	The child may quit too soon without really giving something a try. She may not even start projects. She may not stand up for herself.	The child may be more cooperative in doing things the parents' way, rather than her way. She may have lower stress in life and may be more open to advice and opinions.

Characteristic	Challenges	Benefits
Very Intense **Spirited** Temperament	These children may have a narrow view and be too focused on micro details. They may have a lack of perspective. May have difficulty with emotional regulation and may be volatile and/or find it hard to keep their cool. They may be perceived as too demanding. They are labeled "drama kings and queens."	These children can be very focused, passionate, and make great advocators and leaders. They are enthusiastic, and motivating to others. They are very dramatic and make great actors, teachers, and speakers. They are in tune with other's emotions because they feel the full range within themselves. They display emotions that others find easy to read because they are not subtle.
Even-keeled **Easygoing** Temperament	It may be hard to engage this child and he is often misunderstood as not being interested in things when he is. He may seem careless and unmotivated.	The child is easy to pull away from things and gets over disappointments fast. He can manage his anger easier and is calmer in crisis and conflict situations.
Negative First Reaction **Spirited** Temperament	These children won't go with friends and may miss opportunities. Surprises are not fun for them. They can appear to be aloof and contrary.	These children won't go off with strangers. They are cautious and often plays the "devil's advocate," which brainstorming groups need. They consider safety issues carefully.

Characteristic	Challenges	Benefits
Positive First Reaction **Easygoing** Temperament	This child may be less cautious about safety. She is not always realistic.	This child loves to be surprised. She is somewhat easy to please and parent. She is optimistic, takes on new challenges and looks forward to new things.
High Moodiness **Spirited** Temperament	It can be stressful for others to watch these children's negative moods. It can be difficult for them to get things done. Children are often unpleasant to be with because of unpredictability. It's hard to find peace. Others may not take them seriously, chalking up the issue to "moodiness."	These children become aware of their emotions and learn that feeling their emotions builds skills in handling them and also lifelong resiliency. They are never boring!
Level Emotions **Easygoing** Temperament	This child is less expressive and may be hard to read. He can be perceived as boring, hard-nosed or unfeeling. As an even-keeled person, he may find it hard to understand moody people.	This child has few or mild tantrums. He is very cooperative, predictable and dependable.

Characteristic	Challenges	Benefits
Irregular Body Functions **Spirited** Temperament	These children often don't get enough sleep from night-waking, severe separation anxiety, lateness falling asleep and short naptimes. They have low blood sugar from not eating regularly, but refuses to eat (a result of power struggles when they need food for mood regulation.) Parents feel they need to give some structure to the child and are always on the alert for body needs. It's hard to schedule life without regular sleep and refuelling times.	These children are flexible and can travel easily when nap, meals, and toilet times are not always regular. They have more options and if life gets crazy, they are easily adaptable.
Regular Body Functions **Easygoing** Temperament	It can be hard to meet the needs of the child consistently. Food or nap areas are not always available. It can be a challenge for her to adapt to new environments such as school, sleep-away camp, hospitals, visiting, Grandma's house, etc. It can be difficult for the child to be spontaneous.	The child is organized and prepared. There is a predictable pattern to the day and that gives her and the parents security.

Characteristic	Challenges	Benefits
Very Active **Spirited** Temperament	It's hard to keep these children busy! They are easily bored. As adults, they could become workaholics. They become impatient fast. They don't allow themselves down-time for reflection, contemplation or other activities that spur creativity and thinking. They get frustrated easily with others who live a slower pace.	These children get a lot done as productive older children and adults. They are very energetic and can get by on very little sleep. They are curious and always look for a new adventure or item.
Not Active **Easygoing** Temperament	It can be hard to engage this child in new things or even regular activities. It can be a struggle to keep him fit. Sometimes he just feels lethargic.	This child focuses very easily on his tasks, and he is contented to play on his own. It is not exhausting for parents to keep him constantly occupied or busy. He may like quiet activities such as reading. Home life is more relaxed. He tends to have staying power for long, tedious jobs.

Characteristic	Challenges	Benefits
Very Sensitive (to emotions, clothes, smells, lights) **Spirited** Temperament	These children are often bothered by noise, lighting, fabrics, textures, images, clothing (seams, threads) and smells. The children's feelings can be easily hurt. They complain a lot and have quite a few tantrums. Busy places and crowds of people overwhelm these children and they are very affected by stressful events.	These children are very empathetic and able to "read" the emotional climate of people. Being sensitive people themselves, who feel very deeply, they are keenly aware of other people's feelings and positions and also quite perceptive about typical human behaviour in general. They are compassionate and empathetic and strive to help people in unfortunate circumstances.
Not Sensitive **Easygoing** Temperament	The child is often perceived as being "unfeeling." She often misses other people's feelings and emotions.	The child is easy going, flexible and thinks quite independently. She adapts very quickly to new things and tends to have very black-and-white thinking. She is not very emotionally affected by outside influences.

You are now calm, your child is calm, and because you still have the original problem to solve, you are ready for Step 3.

Step 3
Solve the Problem:
Time Together

STEP 3
SOLVE THE PROBLEM:
TIME TOGETHER

"Anger is a gift that inspires us to change."
~ William Rivers Pitt, Author

Let's go back to the Scott-and-the-chips situation. The floor was covered with crunched chips. I had calmed myself down with Step 1, and managed to get both Scott and his brother calm in Step 2. Now we still have three problems to take care of. We need to first clean up the mess. Next, we need to figure out what to do in the future when someone is angry instead of wrecking the carpet; and lastly, we need to solve the original issue, which was what are acceptable snacks when someone is hungry and someone else is close to serving dinner.

Many times we skip Step 3 as we don't want to bring things up again after everyone is calm. We are scared of rehashing issues in fear of stirring up angry emotions again. Unfortunately, nothing will get resolved if we don't talk.

The whole purpose of anger is to bring issues and problems to the surface in order to resolve them. If people get mad about the issues again, that is their right. Anger affects change. To do this, we need to solve the problem with one of three solutions.

If we avoid issues to avoid people's anger, we get angry because we stuff our resentments. I had to give Scott another way to express his anger because I didn't want the carpet to take another mess and I realized that we still needed to resolve the snack-before-dinner issue.

First things first. We had the issue of the mess on the carpet. We had to solve the problem of how to get it cleaned up. We agreed to vacuum together. He did a four-year-old good-enough job, and I finished up. He sprayed the carpet cleaner and I cleaned it.

Bonus: He learned a new life skill of cleaning carpets.

Second, we had to deal with how he was going to express anger in the future. When we were both calm, we decided on a new way for him to handle his anger. We wrote it on a stickie note and stuck it on the fridge. When he was angry, Scott was going to go to the bathroom, yell into the toilet, and flush his anger away. I would help guide him to this while he was in the middle of anger. We would try this for a week and see if it worked.

Bonus: He learned a new way to express anger that didn't hurt anyone or anything.

Third, we had to deal with the original issue. We negotiated on future treats before dinner. We problem-solved this and agreed that he could have any acceptable treat from a designated drawer in the fridge (that I would stock) before dinner. The treats had to be healthy. We both agreed and solved the problem for next time.

Bonus: We solved our problem and Scott learned three valuable life skills; he learned how to handle anger, clean carpets, and problem-solve an issue. These are all adult life skills. Such learning would not have come had I gave him a spanking, a time-out or a consequence such as taking away computer time.

In our chip scenario, Step 3 took a bit more time. I was calm. My child was calm. But now that everyone was calm, we had two brains to think of future solutions.

You may wish to write this down when dealing with your anger issue:

Considerations

What is the explanation for my child's behaviour?
What is his temperament?
What is his developmental stage?
What are his underlying needs?
What are my needs?
What is my unintended reinforcement?

There are three ways to solve this problem: surrender, leave, or negotiate. Which one should I choose?

For example, using the crunched-chips-on-the-carpet episode, here is what I would write:

What is the explanation for my child's behaviour? Scott was angry because he couldn't have chips before dinner.

What is his temperament? He is a spirited child.

What is his developmental stage? He is a preschooler.

What are his underlying needs? He was hungry. He needed something to eat right away but preferred chips rather than carrots to satisfy his hunger.

What are my needs? I want him to eat nutritious foods to nourish his body. I don't want his hunger at dinner spoiled by eating junky snack foods.

What is my unintended reinforcement? In the past, I have allowed chips because I was tired and couldn't handle a tantrum in that moment. I will try not to do that again no matter how tired I am.

Three Ways to Solve Any Problem

"When my kids become wild and unruly, I use a nice, safe playpen. When they are finished, I climb out."
~Anonymous

There are basically three ways to handle every issue, misbehaviour and parenting problem:

> **A. Surrender**—accept, make a decision to modify the impact on you, live with it, and don't let it affect your enjoyment anymore.
>
> **B. Leave**—dismiss, ignore, get away from the problem.
>
> **C. Negotiate**—converse, collaborate, compromise, problem-solve, fix, make restitution, replace, discuss and work it out so everyone is happy.

I could surrender and let Scott have a few chips. No way.

I could leave the crushed chips up to Dad to clean up. No way. Not fair to my partner.

I could negotiate the chips-before-dinner problem with a four-year-old. Yes.

Let's look at these three options in-depth:

A. Surrender

 "When I was fourteen-years-old, I knew my father was as stupid as a brick. When I turned twenty-one years of age, I was amazed at how much he had learned in the last seven years." ~Mark Twain

Let it go

Is it a discipline problem or a development issue, which they will grow out of? Is it something to worry about or will it eventually take care of itself with just teaching words?

It's helpful to know that children behave in particular ways just because that is the stage of their brain development. Here are the stages of childhood and normal, everyday, typical behaviours. Children develop in four domains at once: physical, cognitive, social and emotional. (Sources in References)

Child Development Stages and Capabilities

Infants   0 to 6 months   Sensory input-output stage

Physical
- Sleeps fifteen to twenty hours in a twenty-four hour period
- Settles into a predictable pattern of eating, sleeping, fussing, and eliminating at three to six months
- Can hold head steady while sitting at four months
- Supports weight of torso with arms while on tummy at three months
- Follows objects and will turn head to look at sounds at two months
- Can transfer objects from hand to mouth at four months
- Teething at five months
- Eats every two hours
- Sits with adult support at six months

Cognitive
- Awareness of sensory input and output; feels cold, so cries
- Doesn't think; just experiences and responds to sensory input
- May become scared of certain faces or sounds

Social and emotional
- Smiles at two months-engages in "serve and return" interactions
- Begins to develop trust and attachment to at least one adult/caregiver
- Crying peaks at two months but remains the main form of communication

Babies   6 to 18 months   Attachment stage

Physical
- Can roll and crawl around seven months
- Supports her own weight when held standing
- Can pull up on tables or chairs to stand at ten months
- Walks around twelve months
- Slithers down stairs backwards at one year
- Takes off clothes at eighteen months
- Runs and climbs at eighteen months
- Sleeps twelve to fourteen hours a night with several daytime naps
- Imitates sounds and babbles
- Says ten to twenty words at eighteen months
- Eats with hands at one year; uses a spoon at eighteen months
- Has most front and side teeth at one year
- Pincer grasp develops

Cognitive
- Explores environment and items with all five senses (mouth, ears, eyes, touch, and hearing)
- No understanding of danger
- No understanding of limits
- No self-control to not do something
- Points to interests
- Develops object permanence at one year; knows something exists even if it can't be seen
- Realizes that he is a separate person around one year
- May understand common words when accompanied by gestures at one year (bye, Mama, ball, shoes)
- Uses words or gestures to express wants by one year
- Is curious; repeats activities to learn
- Short attention span of a minute; is easily distracted

Social and emotional
- Feels happy, sad, mad, surprise, disgust, joy, distressed, and scared
- Has no control of expressing emotions
- Builds security and attachment with attentive adults
- Dislikes strangers beginning at eight months
- Experiences separation anxiety when left by loved adult around ten months
- Fears beginning at one year: animals, thunder, vacuums, theatres

Toddlers   18 months to 3 years   Sensorimotor stage

Physical
- Energetic and active
- Needs meals or snacks every two hours
- Spills and drops
- Can run and climb
- Can use stairs with help
- Opens doors and can press a doorbell
- Needs help with dressing (underwear, socks and shoes); can use shirts and pants
- Can pick up items or throw toys into a bucket
- Can vacuum, sweep and wipe with a cloth
- Sleeps twelve to fourteen hours with one or two naps
- Can drink out of a sippy cup
- Can turn doorknobs and open twist lids at three years
- Can walk down stairs holding a railing at two years
- Feeds self but messy; can use a spoon and perhaps a fork
- Can push a ride-on toy with feet
- Loves to push, pull, fill and empty containers
- Loves physical sensation of materials: goop, Playdough®, food, sand, water
- Can scribble on paper with crayons
- Can throw a big ball with both hands

Cognitive
- Can recognise logos and pictures
- Recognises self and loved ones in photos and mirrors
- No understanding of time
- Can understand that "No!" is a powerful word, but doesn't understand the meaning of "not doing something"
- No idea of danger
- No understanding of tomorrow or yesterday; lives in the moment
- Understands more words than she can speak
- Can say two-word sentences: "More milk," "All gone," "Me go"
- Problem-solves through trial and error; puzzles, shape-sorters
- Doesn't know which objects are breakable and which are not
- Earliest memory from two to three years; remembers moments out of the ordinary
- Can't connect actions with outcomes; doesn't understand consequences
- Labels objects, animals, people, and body parts with names
- Short attention span of a few minutes
- Understands simple directions: "Go get your coat," but may be too engrossed

in play to comply
- No understanding of ownership, money, or sharing
- Explores the world through five senses; needs to touch and taste to learn
- Points to most common objects by name at two years
- Adults can understand 25 to 75% of her speech
- Mixes up "him," "me," "them"
- Can make simple choices between two offerings
- Enjoys repetition of movies, books, rhymes, daily routines, and habits

Social and emotional
- Feelings are intense; feels empathy, frustration, and pride
- Has a favourite cuddly toy that comforts him
- Affectionate to loved ones; loves to cuddle, kiss, pat, sleep with and enjoys being carried
- Excited to see new things
- Becomes stiff or floppy with body when protesting
- Beginning to play with other children, but mostly plays parallel, (side by side) with others
- Tantrums frequent as feelings are overwhelming
- May be contrary; Says "No!" to exert control
- Wants independence to try things and wants to cling to attachment person to build security
- Hoards possessions and people: "Mine!"
- Feels secure in repetition, routines, and familiarity
- Strongly attaches to comforting adults
- Separation anxiety most intense
- Expresses anger and frustration physically and not with words
- Very aggressive: hitting, pushing, biting, and throwing are normal responses
- No self-control to not touch or do things
- Honest
- Night terrors peak at two years

Preschoolers 3 to 5 years Preoperational stage

Physical
- Can jump, kick, swing, skip, hop, run, and throw balls
- Shows intense facial expressions
- Can empty wastebaskets, bring in groceries, mop a floor, spray-clean surfaces, vacuum, pick up socks and library books, set table, help with recycling
- Sleeps twelve hours a night, drops daytime naps
- Can use a toilet independently by four years
- Active, energetic and moves body in coordinated way

- Can hold a pencil and scissors; can print name by five years
- Can fully dress and undress self; uses buttons and zippers
- Can cut food with a knife and use fork and cups; learns to pour
- Can ride a tricycle at three years and a bike with training wheels at five years
- Can brush teeth at five years but needs supervision until eight years
- Less physical and impulsive than toddlers but can still be overcome with emotion

Cognitive
- No understanding of safety considerations or what causes death
- Can't imagine logical outcome of certain actions (operations) on objects or people. Can't foresee consequences
- Intense imagination; magical thinking
- Animism: may have imaginary friends or pets; stuffed animals are "real" to them
- Can't see other's point of view at thee years, but can at five years
- Doesn't understand lying as inappropriate, but as wishful thinking; tells tall tales
- Beginning to connect outcomes with actions (consequences) at five to six years
- Asks a lot of questions; wants to know how things work, including how babies are made; says "What's that?" a lot
- Manipulates objects to learn characteristics
- Stops putting things in his mouth to explore
- Needs to play; gets lost in play and is not distracted by other things
- Adults can understand 75% of speech
- Can say words for everything and use three-word sentences at age three and tell complete stories at age five
- Understands three hundred to one thousand words
- Knows his name and age
- May count numbers and know colors
- Can understand between edible and inedible substances: dirt, shampoo, toilet water
- Unaware of traffic safety; still impulsive
- Can sing, rhyme, and tell jokes
- Able to join in adult-guided problem-solving
- No sense of time or ability to plan; can't understand that adults need to adhere to time schedules; dawdles
- Has nightmares and night terrors
- Longer attention span of about fifteen minutes
- Can follow simple directions: "Put the toy in the box," but compliance still at 40% of the time
- Can recite past experiences but not in the right order
- Begins gender role identification at five years

Social and emotional

- Feels more complex emotions such as jealousy, pride, envy, sympathy, insecurity, and guilt
- Begins to express feelings in words rather than body language of tantrums
- Whines to communicate displeasure
- Imitates adult behaviour
- Enjoys silly and nonsense poems, rhymes, and jokes
- Can be bossy; doesn't understand leadership skills yet
- Feels stress when loved ones are angry
- Anxious to please loved ones
- Power struggles over bedtimes, eating, toileting
- Can share, line up, take turns, compromise, and play cooperatively
- Imagination stirs up fears: animals, dark, carwashes, noises
- May begin tension outlets: nose picking, masturbation, nail biting
- Still has some separation anxiety, especially at night
- May prefer one parent over the other
- Begins to understand that others have different feelings
- Honest and blunt: "Why does your house smell?"
- Enjoys pretend play, role playing, and play dates with other children
- Cooperation increasing but still difficult to stop activities that are enjoyable
- Can delay gratification for five minutes at four years of age
- Tapers off temper tantrums to once a week or less
- Tattles
- Likes to be independent and may refuse help

*Compliance is 40% successful in a respectful, non-punitive parent-child relationship.

Younger School-agers   6 to 9 years
Concrete-operational stage

Physical

- Totally potty trained including night dryness
- Can sleep all night for ten to twelve hours; once asleep, usually stays asleep
- Eats regularly: three meals, three snacks daily
- Can bathe alone
- Can tie shoelaces
- Can ride a two wheeler
- Can use all table utensils including a knife to spread
- Can use cursive writing by nine years
- Loses all baby teeth by eight years

- Can sit still for thirty minutes
- Can stand on one foot and skip
- Bone growth faster than muscle development; may have "growing pains"
- May have nervous habits such as nail biting, hair sucking, masturbation, nose picking, teeth grinding
- Can do most chores with help, direction, and reminding: empty dishwasher, take out garbage, sort laundry, water plants, pet care, meal clean up, recycling, and mopping

Cognitive

- Copycats; loves to imitate others
- Logical; understands that actions have positive or negative outcomes
- Understands operations (consequences)
- Questions; asks "Why?" and "What if?"
- Experiments by trying on behaviours from outside the family
- Rule-focused: loves rules and making sure everyone abides
- Negotiators; loves to make deals
- Concrete learners; understands what she has experienced personally
- Black-and-white thinkers; no gray areas in thinking
- Can work on projects and in groups
- Can sort items into groupings
- Can answer phone but may not take good messages
- Understands clocks and time representation
- Comprehends logical and natural consequences
- Understands that "No" means "Don't do"
- Can recognise ads from various mediums; can differentiate reality from fantasy
- Needs help with homework
- Understands money as a symbol for exchange; can handle an allowance
- Not good enough problem-solvers to stay home alone yet
- Loves new experiences and places: field trips, travel
- Understands jokes; loves potty humour
- Starts reading and writing
- Creative in visual and performing arts and crafts
- Beginning to understand time and the length of a certain block of time
- Can understand the basic mechanics of sexual intercourse and reproduction

Social and emotional

- Protective of belongings and territory
- Sore losers in games due to developing self-control
- Develops definite gender identity as a boy or girl
- May still have fears of dark, animals, sharks, heights, and losing parents
- Understands lying as deceitful and wrong

- Temper tantrums less than once a week if at all; rarely expressed physically
- Learning to recognise other's feelings and able to identify and label his own feelings
- Still hard to see other people's point of view over her own
- Developing social skills of empathy, listening and social "white" lies
- Can begin to use calm-down tools on her own and express anger in words
- Loves to help others and contribute
- Friends come mostly from shared interests
- Still lacks experience in handling conflict
- Good self-control; can wait for ten minutes or longer
- Play is more complex; still enjoys pretend play and loves games
- May prefer same-gender friends
- Not much regard for personal hygiene
- Still open and affectionate with family in public
- Can begin to reflect on own behaviour and how it affects others

*Compliance is 60% successful in a respectful, non-punitive parent-child relationship.

Older School-agers   10 to 12 years

Physical
- May be beginning puberty changes: breast growth, menstruation, height increase. Belt of fat develops around the waist
- Growth spurts and extreme differences are evident in children of the same ages; girls tend to be ahead of boys
- Can mow lawns, do own laundry, wash dishes, cook with microwave, change bedding, answer phone and take messages, pack own lunch, clean bathrooms, and run to the store
- Ravenous appetite or picky eaters or peculiar tastes develop
- Sleeps ten to twelve hours

Cognitive
- Growing out of childhood toys that are becoming boring
- Can use a debit card to make his own purchases
- Needs help with homework and reminding
- Can cross a street alone and judge traffic timing at ten years
- Can stay home alone briefly if good problem-solvers
- Remembers where they left items
- Beginning to resist control by others
- Still black-and-white thinking; moral development progressing with increasing sense of right and wrong

- Attention span of one to two hours
- Knows difference between real and imaginary in digital and physical world

Social and emotional
- Social relationships becoming more complex with feelings and nuances
- Friends mostly come from shared interests; may lose some as interests diverge; sticks to same-sex friends
- Becoming peer focused but family ties still stronger
- May exaggerate and overdramatize problems
- Certain topics, such as sex, are too embarrassing for discussion with family
- Attitude increases as peer behaviour copied
- Learns to handle pressure and rejection
- Worries and anxiety increase as he becomes more self-conscious
- Sensitive to criticism and correction
- May move family affection to private moments

*Compliance is 70% successful.

Younger Teenagers   13 to 15 years
Formal-operational stage

Physical
- Can do all chores physically and intellectually that adults do
- Sleeps nine to ten hours but circadian rhythm pushes bedtime to later in the evening; may be tired from not enough rest
- Can clean the entire house
- Can cook and bake with the oven and stove, and prepare dinner for the family
- Appetite increases
- Puberty changes: menstruation begins, breast growth, curves appear, penis grows, muscles grow, shoulders and hips widen, body hair grows, voice changes, and height dramatically increases
- Girls grow most from eleven to sixteen years of age; boys from thirteen to seventeen years of age
- Hormones in full production; acne appears
- Can be clumsy because bodies are growing inconsistently
- Both sexes eat more
- Permanent teeth are in by age thirteen

Cognitive
- Starting to take full control of homework, school registration, and course choice
- Attention span is the same as adults; good time for visiting museums, theatres, plays, and lectures

- Abstract learners: can understand intangible concepts such as algebra, religion, politics, theories and death
- Can analyse and think critically
- Makes mistakes, decisions and learns from them
- Can make own phone calls and appointments
- Can get around the city on public transit
- Able to understand the rights and responsibilities of owning a smartphone
- Understands values and morals of sexual behaviour
- Needs independence and control over decisions

Social and emotional
- Developing own philosophy, values, and belief systems
- Takes responsibility for her own needs, feelings and behaviours
- Interested in adult conversations
- Physically separates from family to find out who she is but is still emotionally connected; family still matters more than peers
- Can address store and business personnel directly
- Craves independence rather than control by others
- Experimenting with behaviours and substances to handle stress: exercise, alcohol, drugs, internet, social relationships
- Moody
- Impulsive
- Interested in sexuality
- Craves and very protective of privacy
- Lack of confidence saying "No" to others, especially peers
- Very self-conscious
- Peer pressure peaks
- Bullying peaks
- Stops hitting when angry
- Expresses individuality in dress, music, art, and decor that reflects her own values, tastes, beliefs, and preferences
- Explores new identities and roles
- Can babysit younger children

*Compliance is 80% successful.

Older Teenagers   16 to 18 years

Physical
- Have mostly reached adult height, weight, and size
- Brain still changing especially pre-frontal cortex
- Getting wisdom teeth

Cognitive

- Becomes more academically serious
- Can obtain his first job and drivers licence
- Can stay home alone overnight
- Critical thinking blooms; interested in world social, political, economic news
- Can understand mutual funds, Registered Retirement Savings Plans (RRSP), and other financial products and do taxes, and banking
- Sense of omnipotence and grandiosity; believes nothing will hurt them
- Can take full responsibility for school, homework and future planning

Social and emotional

- Anxiety, stress, depression and mental health issues may erupt
- Searching for identity
- Solidifying own values, beliefs, and viewpoints
- Preparing to live in the adult world of work or post-secondary education and living away from home
- Still needs practice in assertiveness skills with teachers, bosses, friends, and service venues
- Needs to prove he is grown up to himself and peers
- Becoming more confident in honouring own values and decisions
- Can stay home alone overnight
- Honing conversation skills

*Compliance is 90% successful.

Emerging Adults   19 to 25 years

Physical

- Same as teenager

Cognitive

- Prefrontal cortex finishes development, which controls adult ability to plan, make decisions, and think critically
- Gaining more common sense

Social and emotional

- Adult stability

* Compliance means that children comply with a directive from a parent in a totally non-punitive parent-child relationship. A non-punitive relationship is one in which no punishments are ever used; instead, active listening, I-statements and problem-solving are used to resolve every discipline issue within an environment of mutual respect and open communication.

Live for today

Now that you know a bit about what children are like at different ages, you may decide that the issue is not about discipline but rather a developmental issue that will get resolved with a gentle teaching word and time. Perhaps you can surrender it.

Parents are often warned to address their child's annoying habit as soon as it pops up. Now that we know about brain development and how children change and can understand more the older they get, we know that annoying habits will not be ingrained. Change is easy later on when everyone is developmentally ready to change.

Until children reach school age, it's important to teach children proper behaviour, but it's important to do so without the expectation that children are going to get it the first time, tenth time, or even the twentieth time. Young children need a lot of practice and repetition. They will get it by the older school-age and teen years.

It's okay to say "No!" That's the hardest part of good discipline. Your child is now going to react, because who likes to be said "no" to? However, here is your job as a parent. Your job is to help your child gain back self-regulation. Also called executive function, self-regulation is the ability to control impulses, even in the heat of anger. It is a critical factor in the success of children's ability to handle disappointment, frustration, and anger.

Many things children do are just what they do. No amount of yelling is going to change the nature of children. It helps to know a bit of brain development. About 40% of all children under the age of five do not comply with parents' first requests. This means that 60% of children do not listen—which is the majority of children that age, and that is perfectly normal! So why get mad about this simple fact of brain development?

B. Leave

If an issue causes you anger and you make a conscious decision to let it go after thinking about it for twenty-four hours, then let it go. Get away from things that make you think of it. Resolve not to give it gas! Remind yourself that you are releasing the issue to the universe and will no longer give it any thought or concern. You will not let it affect you. This too gets easier with practice. If you find yourself still stewing about an issue, especially at four o'clock in the morning, remind yourself over and over that you have decided to let it go. Tangibly write it down and crumple up the paper and throw it away. Do it as many times as you need to in order to remind yourself that you have given this up. As time goes on, it will lessen the impact.

Leaving is not the same as "sulking." One time I was really angry at my partner (well, quite a few times over twenty-five years of marriage!); I didn't speak to him for days. While not speaking to him, the house became quieter as I didn't want to share our normally convivial conversation with anyone, including the children. My kids were aged two to twelve at that time. This year, my adult daughter shared with me how that made her feel. She felt that I was mad at her and the rest of the children. She didn't ask why I was mad at the time and I wasn't very clear about my anger either, so no wonder she felt that way. She also secretly worried that the impasse between her father and I was insurmountable and that we were headed for divorce. Children don't easily share their feelings verbally, but as she got older, she did and it gave me insight that children don't always think the same way we adults do.

Eventually I let go of sulking for days, as it was not nice to do, or nice for others to be around, and certainly not productive. A better plan is to take a brief time-out to express the anger, craft a really good I-statement and then deliver the I-statement to the other person to begin negotiating.

Counteracting parent stress

Parents get so down on each other and themselves, with little in the way of public recognition, but lots in the way of judgment. We need to spread support and a show of appreciation, not judgement, when we see a mom dealing with a toddler tantrum at the playground, a dad with a mouthy teenager in the mall, or a mom with a sulky school-aged child at school. Parenting can be hard, unsupported, and unappreciated work. Yet society needs parents to nurture its next generation of citizens. What job could be more valued? Send three emails to parents you know every day to tell them they are appreciated. Often when I see a parent dealing with a child who is having a tantrum in public, I will go up to the parent and place a $3 coffee gift card in her hand while announcing, "Parenting can sometimes be very hard work. Treat yourself!" What this does is help a parent calm down. It benefits the parent and the child.

Time-off is for Everyone

 "It takes a village—to cherish a parent, to nurture a child."

Everyone needs breaks. Children and parents need some time off for maintenance, to nurture themselves and their relationships.

Ways to counteract parent tiredness

Parent fatigue is a key factor in parent anger. When we are tired everything seems so much worse, from the state of the house, to our child's behaviour. Try to get more sleep.

Here are some tips:

- Sleep when you can. Forget about everything that needs to be done. It won't look so daunting when you are rested, and things will actually get done much faster.
- Ask your partner take the children out so you can nap.
- If you can't sleep, at least try to have some downtime—some quiet to rest and relax.
- Join a babysitting co-op and trade off childcare duties with another mom so you can sleep or get stuff done.
- Accept offers of help and take people up on them. People love to feel needed!
- Demand time for what energizes you: talking on the phone, catching up on social media, reading the newspaper, having a cup of tea or watching a favourite show.
- Use music to relax or energize you. Even the best tunes can spice up a dreary task.
- Know that tiredness won't last forever. Your children will get older and need less supervision, and you can nap more often. Parents report that once their youngest child is about five, they can get much more sleep.
- While children are young, put on a video and do the one-eyed snooze. This is lying on the sofa, dozing, but still being half awake to keep an eye on little ones. Get them to sit beside you so you know where they are. Play the "Sleeping Princess" game where they have to find the prince to kiss you awake and you can rest in the meantime.
- Keep cold. Drink cold water and turn on a fan to keep awake. Soak your feet in a bucket of cold water. It keeps you awake.
- Chew peppermint or cinnamon chewing gum.
- Look at the humour in the situation. It can give you energy.
- Find time to exercise or go for a walk. Fresh air helps to keep awake. Sitting down in a stale-air room will keep you tired.
- Go to a play place with the children and a friend. Stimulating conversation,

laughter and coffee can help keep you awake. Bonus: if you tire the children out enough, you can have a nap when they nap afterward.

- Drinks lots of water. Leave it out on the counter or you won't get around to doing it. A lot of fatigue can be related to dehydration.

- If you are driving home and the children fall asleep, park the car in the driveway with the parking brake on and engine off, and don't disturb them to get them out because they could wake up. Instead, go in the house and grab a pillow. Come back into the car, and snooze in the back seat while they are napping in their car seats. When they wake up, you wake up and can bring everyone in the house.

- If you are driving your older children to activities, still keep a pillow in the car. I often used the time to have a nap and wait for them outside in the car. Of course, this was harder to do with an outside temperature of -25 degrees Celsius!

Start a babysitting co-op

Are you alone in the city with no family or relatives to babysit? Do you need occasional babysitting to get your hair cut, visit the dentist, have a nap, nurse a cold, or enjoy an evening out with your partner? Perhaps a babysitting co-op is the answer.

To find a babysitting co-op in your area, check the community centers, parent time-out groups, or churches to see if one already exists. If not, check with other moms at the playground while you are supervising your children. Many co-ops exist by word of mouth only.

If your community doesn't have one, it's easy to start. All you need is another mom and some agreed-upon rules, tokens, and structure. Here are some considerations:

1. Numbers: Aim for about ten to twelve families. Not too big that you don't know everyone and not too small that you run out of phone numbers before you find a commitment to babysit your children when needed.

2. Tokens: Use wood disks, poker chips, or painted coins. Many co-ops start with thirty hours allocated to everyone to begin, and everyone leaving has to hand in thirty hours.

Tokens are made in different colors to represent one hour and one-half-hour tokens. In my co-op, we pay one token per hour for the first child and a quarter token for each additional child in the family, per each additional hour. That way, larger families are not penalized too much. Some co-ops charge a half token for second and subsequent children.

3. Rules: Keep the rules to a minimum, and make sure that all charter members agree to them. Some general considerations are that the mother is the one babysitting, unless otherwise agreed to. During the day, the children to be babysat are transported to the babysitter's house. In the evening, the babysitter comes to the children's house to sit and puts the children to bed in their own domain. Meals, transportation, and outings are negotiated between the two parties. A discipline policy should definitely be discussed at the charter member meeting. Communication is important so misunderstandings are avoided.

4. Structure: Some co-ops have a secretary that one could phone to request a babysitter. The secretary would then phone the lowest token holder first to babysit and go down the list if needed. The secretary position is rotated monthly. Other co-ops have each person do her own phoning for babysitting, which has the advantage that the person can choose who the child likes to play with the most. Generally, the person with the lowest number of tokens should be phoned first. Regardless of structure, members should meet monthly on a rotational basis at each others' houses to discuss token counts, arrange future sits, and problem solve any issues that come up. Moms really look forward to the monthly meeting, as it's a social visit and support group also!

The advantages of babysitting co-ops are numerous. To children, they are like a play date with their friends. Often, babysitting other children helps keep yours occupied, and you as the babysitter can get more done too! It's inexpensive and parents have the security of knowing that an adult is in charge rather than a teen. Many moms like to babysit at another's house in the evening, as they are free to do some quiet work, read, or enjoy a hobby once the children are in bed—things they wouldn't otherwise get done in their own home. Perhaps the most compelling advantage is that the social and support network of similar-aged children and parents is wonderful to have in this day of isolated nuclear families.

Time for yourself

One of the toughest things a parent or anyone in a close relationship faces is giving herself permission to take a time-out for herself—personal satisfaction time. Don't feel guilty; it's a necessity. Schedule regular time so everyone in the family gets used to it and it becomes non-negotiable. Mom could take a few hours on Saturday and Dad on Sunday to do whatever each wishes to do. If a parent is single or the other partner travels a bit, try swapping childcare with another parent or set up a babysitting co-op. Or try to schedule in personal time through the week while the children are occupied in the house. What could you do in five minutes, twenty minutes, or two hours? Make a list:

Five minutes: check e-mail or a social media update, enjoy a cup of tea, go outside for a breath of fresh air, go to the bathroom alone, or open mail.

Twenty minutes: read a magazine article, watch a bit of TV, have a quick bath or shower, talk to a friend on the phone, or read the newspaper.

Two hours: go out if you have childcare, nap, take a bubble bath, or watch a movie at home. Don't clean, organize, or do chores! This is time to nurture you, not the house!

Sometimes children need about ten or twenty minutes of your focused time to fill up on attention and will then leave you alone for some time to yourself. They will engage in a solitary playing activity. However, if you force them to leave you alone when they are lacking attention, they probably won't leave you alone because they are still low on attention needs. Giving attention is the best way to solve this, rather than punishments or harsh words.

Examine your "to do" list with a critical eye and choose only those items that absolutely have to get done that day to meet your families needs. Trim everything off the list. They will get done eventually. If you are a type "A" driven person, move the items off the list today to another day on your calendar so you can know that they will get done eventually.

Put Dad to work. Outings Dad could take children to: grocery shopping, pet stores, hardware stores (children love the escalators and ceiling fans), errands, playgrounds, parks, picnics, bike riding, and sports events. My children's favourite was just riding the city train, with no particular destination in mind.

Try to aim for a good night's sleep every night. Half of all discipline problems could be solved if only parents had a good night's sleep. Meet your needs for meals and water. Many moms don't drink enough water and feel tired and dehydrated. When you feel better, minor irritations of parenting, such as a toddler's tantrum, affect you less because you are in a better space.

Time off for couples

In the movie *Date Night*, the characters played by Steve Carell and Tina Fey are in a long-term relationship that they try to spice up by going out to dinner once a week on a date night. The trouble is that their date night is monotonously predictable:

they go to the same restaurant and order the same food on the same night. They start to notice the sameness when they become a little too clichéd even for their own taste by talking about the variation of the chicken quality instead of their feelings, week after week. One night they do something different—they dress up, pick a new restaurant, and go to dinner in the city for a change. What happens next is hilarious and they end up with an incredible evening tale—probably one that no couple would wish for—but the end result is that they had a renewed sense of each other as the people they loved, not just in their roles as parents dealing with children and siblings, although those roles were strengthened as well.

No matter how long they have been together, couples need sparks, creativity, and fun in their relationship. As the years pass, they need it even more. For centuries, organized religion has discovered that people need continuous affirmation of their faith in the form of weekly rituals such as church attendance. Relationships need the same kind of nurturing and care. Regular meetings are required in order to talk, have fun, and spend time together. We know that friendships survive on shared interests, yet as soon as we partner up with our very best friend, we tend to settle into domestic boredom and let the shared interests slide. Every relationship has peaks and valleys—moments where love is overwhelming and moments when you seriously wonder why you are still with him or her. Couples need to remind themselves of the qualities that attracted them to each other at the beginning of the relationship, and what they still love about each other. This is even more critical when mortgages, pets, children, jobs, laundry, broken appliances, normal conflicts, and elderly caretaking occur alongside the couple relationship. These are normal stresses, but they can be overwhelming in a relationship without some nurturing buffers, such as date night and time together.

Research shows that the first five years of a relationship are the most difficult because of career-building demands, money woes, and especially the parenting of babies and toddlers. The lack of sleep, child tantrums, worry, and differing parenting styles can tear down the closeness and caring of even the most loving of couples as we tend to take our parenting frustrations out on each other rather than the children. This can be toxic to relationships. (Thomas, 2013) We need frequent reminders to be kind and caring to each other, in the good times and especially in the challenging times. As kids get older and easier to parent, relationships naturally improve, but take a dip again in the children's teen years. This coincides with menopause, career peaks, travel, and midlife crisis issues. The parenting of teens can be challenging and adds to the stress. Couples need to put more work into their relationship at this stage, similar to the first five years. Research shows that as children reach the adult stage, parental relationships improve and enrich. That's a no-brainer, because parenting is very much "done." As parents move into the parent-adult child relationship stage, parenting is very enjoyable and rewarding as the children become your new best friends.

We started our own date night when we had three children under three and felt we were losing the essence of "us" in the dreary day-to-day details of domestic life. We made a point of hiring a babysitter to come every Tuesday evening for our standing date night. Some days we were so tired we blearily welcomed in the sitter, grabbed our pillows, and headed to the parked car in the driveway for a blissful, uninterrupted nap. People would question the cost of a standing sitter, but we considered it a financial investment. Research shows that divorce is the single most disastrous event that devastates a couple's finances and wealth, (Brown, 2013) and in light of that we felt that hiring a weekly sitter made sound financial sense. Not only did we fund her college education, but the kids actually enjoyed the sitter coming, since we didn't have any grandparents or relatives to help out. She was fun, responsible, and became an extended family member. The kids loved the new video games she brought each week.

It was hard when the young babies and toddlers were going through separation anxiety. Although we are both attachment parents, their crying seemed to bother me more than my partner. I would like to say the decision was easy, but like many gray areas in life, sometimes I felt that I couldn't leave the kids and so I discussed with my husband some ways to stay at home and not leave them, and he was sensitive to my needs. Other times I realized his needs had to come first and we absolutely needed some time alone for the sake of our relationship or we might not make it through another week. We would desperately say goodbye to the kids as gently as we could and walk out the door. Like any relationship, we had to determine whose needs were paramount at that moment, and meet them. That's real life. The kids usually had settled in with the sitter by the time we phoned ten minutes later, and most often we had a great evening, a heartfelt talk, and the kids were okay. We felt that a strong parenting partnership was in the greater good for all concerned in the long run. As is many parenting decisions, when and how to leave the children is a decision that each couple must make and decide what is best for them.

We felt a critical aspect of parenting was giving the kids a role model for respectful relationships and a blueprint for keeping love, passion, and companionship alive in long-term, monogamous relationships, whether that followed a traditional husband-and-wife marriage or domestic partnership between consenting, loving adults of any gender. We try to hash out conflicts in front of the kids, as well as resolve and make up, too. We need to show them that parents are humans, too.

In addition to date night, we also have private time on our own. We have Mom's night out (where Mommy goes to the movies or book club with her friends) and Dad's day out (where Dad goes out to play volleyball with his friends). People need to care for themselves in order to care for others.

Twenty-five years later, we are still going strong. With five children, some of who are teens and adults, we no longer need babysitters. Spontaneity is back. We can suggest a movie to each other and be out the door in five minutes, just like we did BC (before children). We even put some friendly daring into the mix—once we parked in the expectant parent's parking spot at the movie theatre and then ordered the seniors' rate movie tickets to get in! We didn't tell the kids!

"Date night" rules

Together, choose an evening of the week for date night, but make it consistently the same day of the week or it will get left by the wayside. If you have children, hire a regular sitter to come each week at the same time. Try to find a sitter who drives and pay the sitter well. If finances are a problem, join a babysitting co-op and trade tokens. If separation anxiety is a problem, plan date nights at home when the children are asleep. Each partner takes a turn planning the date, executing, driving, and paying. The other partner is the guest. Then the next week, switch roles. It's more fun to keep plans a secret until you are both in the car or it's time for the date. Surprise is part of the fun! The planner should hire the sitter and feed the kids before you go out. Look your best, even for home dates. The only information the guest needs to know is what to wear and if they should eat before going out. Try to plan an evening without friends, so that intimate subjects can be addressed if need be. Some subjects are difficult to bring up, but with time and space, it's better to broach the subjects and give it airtime than to bury it. Couples who bury critical conversations end up with nothing to talk about in the later years and can drift apart. Be tolerant and enjoy the evening as much as possible, knowing that your partner put a lot of effort into making it special for you, even if he didn't quite nail it that week.

For more ideas that are continually updated, visit our blog, Date Night YYC (www. datenightyyc.ca). Even though the ideas are for Calgary and the surrounding area, they are easily transferable to any city. If you have young children, check out the blog for information on how to start a babysitting co-op.

"Date night out" ideas

- Live theatres (high schools and smaller troupes have inexpensive or no-cost nights)
- Concerts (check out university and community bands)
- Parks and reserves offer boating rentals
- Go out for a coffee or a beer at the local pub
- Picnics everywhere
- Dinner crawl—go to several restaurants, having at appetizer at one, salad at another, entrees at another, and dessert at another

- Pub hopping downtown
- Zoo, museum, library or science centre
- Wine-tasting events
- Couple's massage
- Pottery painting
- Classes
- A friend's house party
- Go out for breakfast or meet for lunch
- "Lovers or couples" trade show
- Comedy theatre, Pecha Kucha, MoMondays
- Bike ride; either bikes or motorcycles
- Drive-in movie or movie-in-the-park
- Pick up take-out and watch the planes land at the airport
- Go-carting or laser tag
- Shakespeare or other plays "in the park"
- Fitness: gym date, bowling, rock climbing, yoga, roller skating, golf, hiking, or simply running
- Lectures (check out libraries, universities, and bookstores)
- Volunteer together such as canvassing, working at the food bank, and places where you can talk and have fun
- Window shop
- Ride the city trains—bring a snack and have a train picnic

"Date night in" ideas

- Snuggle in bed with a movie and a picnic of wine, bread, and cheese
- Dinner and movie at home with a theme such as French night—have crepes, cheese and a charcuterie platter and watch a French film
- Board or card-game night
- Dance
- Bake cookies
- Play video games
- Read together in the bathtub, with candles, bath salts, and wine
- Grab a pillow, blanket and sleep in the car with the baby monitor on
- Pick up books from the library and have a read-in around the fireplace
- Sit around the fire pit outside and make marshmallows or hot dogs
- Relax in the hot tub
- Be a kid again and use the trampoline (or just lie on it and watch the stars), swing set, or swimming pool
- Turn off all the lights, sit in the dark and watch the animal world outside
- Bring out photo albums or watch photos and videos on the big screen at home

"Date night no-sitter-available" ideas

- Car rides and walks (kids will either fall asleep or be entertained by the DVD player you bring).

- Go to places like Ikea, McDonalds, airports, and children's hospitals. Grab a coffee and a bench and utilize the play places to keep your kids entertained where you can talk but keep an eye on the children.

- Go to a bookstore and plunk the kids in the children's section with an assortment of books. Grab an in-house coffee and find a nearby seat.

- Set the alarm early and have coffee on the porch and watch the sun come up together.

- Take the kids to the playground and have a picnic for you two.

- If your kids are school-aged, book two tables at a restaurant at least ten yards apart. Sit your kids at one table, and you and your partner at another. Monitor them from afar. Pretend you are the aunt and uncle so you don't worry about their behaviour. This works even better with teens.

Couple time instead of date night

If date night is not your cup of tea, it might be important to set aside fifteen minutes a day for couple time instead of a formal date time. Grab a cup of tea or glass of wine and head to a quiet place, such as the sofa, the deck, the front porch, the bedroom—even the bathroom if you have to. We used to take the children to the park and talked together while sitting on the park bench. Try to talk about feelings, opinions, and values rather than just the details of life running smoothly. Instead of, "Will you pick up the dry-cleaning tomorrow?" try, "How did you feel when you were rushed at work today? That must have been hard for you."

Try to keep one room in the house that is a retreat space—one room with no toys or clothes lying around. Perhaps it could be a hobby room, office, guest room, workshop, or sewing room.

Begin taking couple time when children are toddlers. By the time they are school-aged, they will get used to waiting for Mom and Dad's attention for a short period of time. Of course, toddlers and preschoolers are a bit young to understand how to wait, but definitely by school-age, children can estimate what 15 minutes is and give you both some space.

When your partner comes home from work; having her or him spend time with the children helps in filling up their attention needs, so the children will give you both some time.

Find time to connect throughout the day. Kiss and hug at every goodbye. Touch and cuddle whenever you can especially while talking to each other. Phone each other at work. Send flowers for no reason. Write a note on the baby's diaper to give to your partner when he changes the baby next. Leave notes on pillows and in lunches. Spontaneous or planned signs of appreciation keeps the love flowing!

Do this all in full view of the children. They often see us yell at each other, and need to see us show affection and love too. If they say, "Get a room!," you know they might be embarrassed outwardly, but are happy inwardly that they still have parents who love each other.

The greatest gift you can give your children is a loving parenting partner in a secure couple relationship. For some date night ideas, visit **www.datenightyyc.ca**

Time with each child

Spend time with each child often enough so each child will feel special. Let her lead the activity. Have no other siblings along. In our house, we used the birthday date to allocate special time. My son was born on September 4, so every fourth of the month is his "special date" to pick an activity he wanted to do with Mom, Dad or both. We booked off all the dates a year ahead, so we knew not to plan any other activity those evenings.

In the early days, with my partner working out of town, I would get a sitter to stay with the other kids. It's amazing the difference in our parent-child communication because of this practice, and how much it cuts down on sibling fighting.

Now that the kids are teens, I am no longer allowed to call our special time "date night" but we do keep the date in our respective calendars as "time off with Mom (or Dad)."

De-clutter Your Life

Too much stuff, obligations, and people can make our lives stressful and leave us with a short fuse of anger. We need to occasionally do some pruning. Your children need more of you; they don't need more stuff, activities, and other people. Streamline your life so you can give more of yourself to your children, without the stress caused by too many competing interests.

Your stuff

Material stuff is nine times less important to happiness than personal resources, such as family relationships, friendships, contributing to others' lives, and celebrating life events. Most storage is procrastination of decision-making. Where do I put this stuff? What do I do with it? Or, if you have an idea of what to do with it, you have no time to put it in action and keep putting it off. How many broken items are stored with the best intentions of fixing them?

Often we search for new and bigger houses or renovate for more storage space when really we should be going through our stuff and pruning it. Keep what we need for our life today. Most people store too much stuff. Only 20% of the house should be allocated to storage, including bookcases, dressers, closets, cupboards, shelf, and storage containers.

An organized house reduces your stress level. No, you don't have to get rid of everything, as my husband often fears! Just keep what you love and use. There are many great books in the library to help you streamline your house.

Your relationships

When people look at de-cluttering, they tend to focus on objects. They also need to focus on the cluttering people in their lives. By de-cluttering people, I mean we need to examine all the relationships in our lives and prioritize and redirect our energies to those relationships that give us pleasure. I'm not saying you have to dump your partner because he annoys you from time to time. I'm saying we need to look at the equity in our relationships. All give or all take is not healthy for you or the other person. It's not fair to you when you give 95% and receive 5% back. We have to re-evaluate those ties that we maintain only out of a sense of obligation and duty. And yet, they take up so much time and energy that we could use to make our lives less stressful.

For example, when Aunt Martha calls (and we all have someone like Aunt Martha in our lives) and complains for two hours daily about her aches and pains, all the bad things that have happened to her, everything that's gone wrong in her life, and she spends five minutes listening to how you are, it's not fair. You can feel the life energy being sucked right out of you. You hang up feeling like a limp balloon.

Then you take your annoyance out on your toddler by getting angry because he just spilled his juice. Establish a boundary there. Give Aunt Martha five minutes of your most focused, empathetic listening, and then say, "Sorry, I have to go now."

Moods are contagious. Associate with positive people and you will have a more positive outlook on life. When we surround ourselves with people who nurture us, they feed our ability to nurture others. Drop the "should's" and "ought to's." Focus on the people in your life that really matter to you, who are kind to you, who give you nurturing, support, and affirmations. Who do you want to make more time in your life for?

Your obligations

De-cluttering your obligations requires prioritizing and redirecting your energies to those things you really want to do with your life.

You should love your work 80% of the time. If not, redirect your energies to what you really want to be doing. If you had five years left to live, would you be doing what you are doing today? A friend once told me that you should find out what you love to do and then find someone to pay you to do it. If you can, turn a hobby into a business.

Drop the should's and ought to's and cut down on your commitments. When we rush from activity to activity, we become stressed and lose our patience. Who do we take it out on? Often our children. It hit me one day, while serving a fast-food lunch to four children in the back of the van: I was trying to navigate the fastest road in our city with the fries flying in the back seat. You could have heard me yelling all the way across the city when the ketchup dripped all over the upholstery. Too much to do and no time to do it. Rush, rush, rush!

Slow down. Life becomes so much easier at a "child's pace." Instead of saying, "Hurry up, we're late," say "That's okay, take the time you need." Seriously look at what needs to be cut down or out in order to slow your adult pace. Do children really need all those extra-curricular activities or do they need a peaceful family life and a parent who doesn't yell all the time?

Learn to say "no." When you do add a new activity, drop one you are no longer interested in as much, so you keep a flow-through calendar rather than just adding and adding. Keep in mind to add driving and preparation time to activities. A one-hour meeting can really take three hours out of our day when those factors are considered. To keep balance in our lives, we need reflection and downtime as much as we need activity. What do you want to make more time for?

Does baking homemade cookies for your child's class, offering to coordinate the yuletide pageant, or sitting on a school committee really benefit your child directly in terms of one-on-one, direct attention time? No. These types of commitments eat into the time with your child. You must step back and really examine the reasons you are doing these things. Is it for your needs or your children's? It is adding or reducing stress to the family? Is this the time in your life that is appropriate for this type of commitment or would another stage of life be better? Some things might have to go on the back burner. There are good causes, but maybe it's time for someone else to step up and volunteer. Think about your children, you, and your partner. Is this best for all of you right now?

Do some serious life de-cluttering and you will reap the benefits. You will have more time, patience and energy for the people you love, the things you love to do, and more space to do it in. Feel the exhilaration, the sense of freedom, the enjoyment of a lighter load! It's worth it.

Work or play?

There I am sitting on the floor of my four-year-old and five-year-old sons' bedroom, and I am happily, contently, and blissfully absorbed playing parking lot with rows of Lego® and little metal cars. Then I spot it. Dirt! I see a ledge that I have never seen before from this angle. How often do you see your house from the point of view of a small child? It was disgusting! A ledge full of five years worth of dust, grime, and grease that has never seen a dust cloth. I abruptly changed from my blissful state into a panic, consumed with guilt, because I really should not be playing with toys when dirt is silently breeding in little nooks and ledges. It was almost enough to ruin a perfectly wonderful day of enjoying my children. I could just hear the tape of society's expectations playing in my head: a good mother has a spotless house. A good mother has everything in place and has perfectly clean children. She herself must look exquisite. Dinners must also be cooked nutritiously and homemade. STOP!

It was time to replay the messages in my head. Besides, I love playing Lego®, the children love playing with me, and my partner loves us all in a happy mood, so if I had to endure a dusty ledge in my face while doing it, then so be it! Over the years, I have collected poems and quotes for my fridge that help alleviate the "dirty house" guilt. Here are some:

"Our home is clean enough to be healthy and dirty enough to be happy."

"If you want to see my house, please make an appointment; if you want to see me, please come on in!"

"No one says on their deathbed, 'I wish I had a cleaner house.'"

Sign on the front lawn, "I'm not growing grass, I'm growing children."

The housework will always be there. The children grow up so fast.

C. Negotiate

Positive discipline can only take place after the child and parent are calm. Both can think straight and solve the problem that the anger was about. If anger was out of control this time, discuss what calm-down tool to try next time. Pick a new one from the list in Step 2.

In the example of Scott crunching the chips into his carpet, we talked about what to do with his anger next time instead of smashing chips. We agreed to try "throwing his stuffies at his bed." We wrote this down on a post-it note and put it on the fridge. By putting it on the fridge, which is opened more than once a day, chances were good that it would be embedded in his sub-conscious. Next, we had to clean up the chips on the carpet. He and I vacuumed them up together. He sprayed the carpet cleaner on it and both of us got a rag and cleaned the carpet. Being four, he wasn't very good at cleaning up, but that didn't matter. It was the act of contributing to the "making good" that was important. He learned how to clean carpets, how to fix things and how to be responsible for one's actions. He learned the "adult way."

Natural consequence checklist

- If you break it, fix it.
- If you use it, put it back.
- If you lose it, replace it.
- If you need it, ask for it.
- If you damage it, repair it.
- If you drop it, pick it up.
- If you make a mess, clean it up.
- If you promise it, follow through.
- If you hurt it, make amends.

Once the carpet was cleaned, we discussed the original problem. He was hungry before dinner. We problem-solved it by discussing my needs for him to not spoil his appetite before dinner and his needs to eat. We brainstormed some reasonable healthy foods and agreed to make a list of snacks that were healthy and that he liked. Chips were not on the list.

We dealt with the presenting problem by problem-solving. It is the one great positive discipline tool that is respectful and gets at the true issue. I could have solved the problem of the not-listening and the defiance of grinding the chips into the carpet by any number of ways: spanking, giving him a time-out, or taking away video game time for the next week. However, none of those options would have taught him good food choices, why my needs for him to not spoil his appetite were important, and how people clean up messes. He learned those things through his mess clean up follow-through and our mutual problem-solving.

Collaborative Problem-solving

Problem-solving is simply conversing with your child or children on the topic of a problem and engaging them to help out with solutions. It's not just the parent figuring out how to solve the problem. It is the parent and the child working together against the problem. It works for people from ages three to ninety years and beyond.

Seek first to understand by active listening

In speaking to parents and families about problem-solving, the most common concern is that it is hard to fine-tune what the problem is and what people's needs are. Parents must get into the habit of truly understanding what the child is feeling or needing instead of focusing on what they are going to say next. Listening and observing will clue them into what the real deal is. Acknowledging feelings is helpful. Once parents know what the real issue is, they can check that out with the child.

Active listening or acknowledging feelings occurs when the parent tries to understand what the child is **feeling** and the **content** of her message, both verbal and nonverbal. The parent then puts her understanding into her own words and feeds it back to the child. This is very useful when a child has a problem. Validation and acknowledgement of feelings doesn't mean agreement. It only means truly accepting where the person is emotionally. It also serves to help the child clarify why she was angry. It finds the underlying emotion and pinpoints exactly what the issue was about.

"Sounds like you are **frustrated** because _____"

"I can see you might be feeling **angry** because_____"

"You're feeling **sad** when _____"

"It sounds as if you feel **disrespected** by the way **I talked to you when you came home last night**."

For example, a child keeps pinching her sibling when the parents are not looking. By actively listening to the child the parent can say, "You seem to be annoyed by your sister and express that by pinching her. Do you feel that she gets more attention and time with us than you do?" A parent can get a picture of what is going on because it starts the conversation. The key is listening without judgment. Sure, it is not right that the child pinches her sister, but perhaps she has real concerns, such as not getting enough attention. When the attention issue is taken care of, the pinching will stop.

Active listening (or acknowledging feelings) help you understand their point of view.

Declare your unhappiness by using I-statements

Now it's your turn. I-statements help other people understand your point of view. They are much more respectful than You-statements and they let someone know that you have a problem with her behaviour. An effective I-statement has three parts that communicates your **feeling**, the specific descriptive **behaviour**, and the **reason** to the person.

> "I feel **demoralized** when I see the **kitchen is a mess**, because **I have to spend time cleaning it up.**"

> "I feel **frustrated** when I hear **siblings bickering** and **I can't concentrate on my work.**"

> "I'm **worried** that **jumping on the sofa** will damage the springs and **I will have to pay for a big repair bill.**"

The problem-solving process

Once you understand the other person's point of view through active listening, and she understands your point of view through your I-statement, then you both can move into solving the problem.

Let's again use the scenario of Scott crunching the chips into the carpet.

Step 1 Determine the problem. Scott is hungry.

Step 2 What are my needs as a parent? I need him to eat nutritious foods.

I declare these in an I-statement. "I **worry** that you will get sick **when you don't eat healthy foods** because then **I will have to take time off work to get you to the doctor.**"

What are my child's needs? He wants chips to resolve his hunger. I find this out by actively listening to his feelings. In the problem-solving model, a child's needs and wants are all the same to him. Children don't understand the difference and will behave to get what they want, regardless of what adults label it. I would acknowledge his feelings by saying, "Are you **hungry** and want something delicious to eat? You were **angry** when I wouldn't allow you the chips."

Step 3 What are some possible win-win solutions that Scott and myself came up with?

- Mom could set aside a drawer in the fridge or cupboard of acceptable snacks that Scott could have.

- Mom could agree that Scott could have five chips and then fill up with crackers and cheese.

- Mom and Scott could agree that he could have a vegetable tray and when that is gone, fill up on chips.

- Mom could decide not to buy the chips and bring them into the house.

- Scott and Mom come up with more ideas...

Step 4 Evaluate all ideas. For us, all the above worked okay.

Step 5 Pick an idea that both parties agree to. We agreed to the special cupboard of snacks chosen by Scott and Mom.

Step 6 Check back and see if it is working for both of us. We agreed to try it for a week and see if it worked for both of us. We got to work to set up the cupboard.

We also chose a new method for Scott to express his anger during the week. He decided he was going to stomp to his room and cry. I agreed that I would notice and see what was wrong with him when he did that and come up to offer him comfort when he was angry.

See the Appendix for a Problem-solving Template that you can copy and fill out.

Positive Discipline

Two of the most anger-producing behaviours in children that set parents' anger off are deliberately disobeying and not listening.

How to deal with "deliberate disobedience"

Get calm first. You can't deal with this effectively when you are livid. Then, declare your I-statement to your child and start problem-solving the situation. If your child is shoplifting after you told her not to, you have to get to the bottom of why she is doing it by active listening and then come up with win-win solutions.

What is her need or feeling that she is shop-lifting? Is she acting out of peer-pressure? Does she really need the item? Does she see no other way to get her needs met? Coming up with solutions together to solve the underlying need or feelings (and of course making amends with the store) is far more effective in the long run than punishing the child by grounding or consequences. And it keeps the relationship intact.

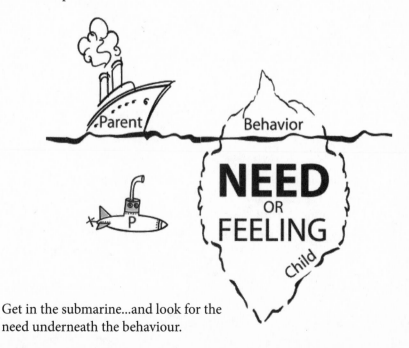

Get in the submarine...and look for the need underneath the behaviour.

How to deal with "not listening"

- Ask yourself if it is age-appropriate. Is the child too busy or distracted to listen? See the section on child development stages in Step 2.

- Go directly up to your child and whisper in your child's ear.

- Or go directly up to your child, get down to her level so you can get eye contact, state your request, and put your hand on her shoulder and stay there until she complies.

- Declare your feelings, "I'm feeling really angry. I'm frustrated that you are fighting. I'm angry that nothing is happening and I don't wish to yell."

- Don't talk at all. Just do what you need to do. You can only control yourself, not your child. Stop doing things, change things around or take action. If your daughter doesn't clear the washer for you to use it and she wants you to drive her somewhere, just tell her that you had an extra twenty minutes but it was taken up by clearing out her laundry. Just do it!

Begin with a hug and comfort

The children who need the most love are sometimes the ones who ask for it in the most unloving way. If in doubt about what to do, start with a hug. It calms everyone down and they can begin solving the problem from a place of connection. And no, it doesn't teach kids to act up in order to get a hug. Kids don't manipulatively think of ways to act up. Their emotions are raw, instant and intense. Giving a hug to help them calm down is the fastest way to comfort them and get to the heart of the problem.

Unless you are the problem, and then they won't want the hug. But that's okay!

What is punishment?

Punishment includes physical punishments such as spanking, slapping, pushing, and pinching. It also includes emotional punishments such as jail-time parent-forced time-out, parent-imposed (logical) consequences, taking away items and privileges, and shaming. If you are not sure, ask your children. They will tell you what is punishment and what is not. They have an uncanny sense of fairness.

What is not punishment?

Childproofing, problem-solving, safe natural consequences, and time-in are not punishments. Problem-solving that includes fixing, repair, restitution, remuneration, or making amends is not a punishment but realistic, adult methods to solve a real problem or relationship issue. Consequences can be punitive if parents impose them against the child's protests and there are other ways to fix the problem instead of consequences designed to hurt the child, "teach a lesson," and not solve the problem. If you still can't tell if your "outcome" is punitive, then a good rule of thumb is the "partner test." If you wouldn't do it to your partner, (or friend, mother-in-law, neighbor, boss, colleague) then don't do it to your child.

Why can't I use punishment?

When parents use punishment on children, they may get compliance in the short run, and studies do show this, but it affects the parent-child attachment, ease of communication, increased anger, and the relationship.

When research indicates that certain techniques gain obedience from the child, it is deemed that the techniques are successful. However, since research doesn't quantify the quality of parent-child relationships, many "well-researched" programs may lead to dismal parent-child relationships. (Arnall, 2014)

There are absolutely no research or studies that show that punishment enhances parent-child relationships. There are many studies that show it has a detriment to it. (Gordon, 2000)

And it gets worse as children get older. Obedient children stay like that until they become bigger, stronger, and more capable and powerful in the teen years. That is when parents lose their teen's respect, compliance, companionship, and conversation. When teens are punished, parents get anger in the form of attitude, sarcasm, apathy, rudeness, and rebellion. (Gordon, 2000)

Teens that are not punished report open, close, fun, and caring ties with their parents. No topic is off the table when they converse. Parents are free to share their opinions and experience, and teens listen. In our digital world, more than ever children need their parents' open communication and nurturing as a lifeline to navigate complex situations. They need someone with life experience who is on their side to confide in. I did not use physical punishment, but did dabble in time-outs, and logical consequences for punishing my children because most of the 350 parenting books I read told me that it was the only approach. Apparently 85% of parents punish their children when they misbehave. The 15% of parents that don't ever use punishment still have great kids. (Gordon, 2000) When my oldest sons were ten and nine, I realized that using consequences was affecting our relationships in that they were starting to stop talking to me. I decided to stop all punishments. From then on, we dealt with all "conflicts" or "discipline issues" by problem-solving. It worked so well, I never used any punishment on the two youngest children. All my children have never been grounded, had their phones or computers taken away, or had punitive consequences imposed.

The teen years were a breeze and the young adult years are even better. We have open communication. We share feelings and problems. Growing up, the kids even chose to spend family time together over peer time, and we had many wonderful family-oriented activities. We did not hear a shred of "attitude." They didn't smoke, binge drink, vandalize, steal, do drugs or talk back. Over all, they were pretty responsible kids. You really don't have to punish children to have wonderful kids. Why not give it a try for a year and see the result in a closer relationship with your child?

Cancel the consequences in the teenage years

Do you want your teen to:

- Share their thoughts, feelings, problems and worries with you in a real, meaningful conversation without attitude and sarcasm?
- Do chores and pitch in on family projects without being asked?
- Enjoy family activities and want to spend time with you?
- Be responsible and accountable to their studies and their jobs?
- Solve their problems by discussion rather than avoiding them by drinking, sex, gambling, and drugs?
- Care about your feelings, needs, and worries and modify their behaviour in response?

This is not utopia. Many families already enjoy this kind of relationship with their teens. However, the one factor that promotes this kind of parent-teen relationship is completely dropping all punishments.

I teach parents of teens good communication skills. Many parents wonder why their teens don't talk to them even when they "try" the communication skills of active listening. I ask if they use "consequences" as discipline. I have never had a "no" answer in 18 years of teaching parenting classes.

The simple answer is that teens are not stupid. They simply don't open up to parents who want an open relationship in terms of sharing conversation, but then promote a closed relationship in terms of punishing their children. Parents can't expect openness in one area when they hurt their child in another area. I know that parents mean well and love their children; but they cling to age-old parenting methods that may have been appropriate 30 years ago when children had a community to supervise them. Parents are now parenting in the digital age. The internet places new challenges in family life and parents can't afford to lose their open communication lines with their children. Supervision is difficult to do with the anonymous nature of the internet, and parents must rely on their open communication with their children to guide them and keep them safe. We live in a different world and parents can choose methods of teaching that are non-punitive but still have structure and nurturing.

We tell parents not to use physical punishments anymore. As a result, many parents don't spank. However, many parents of young children now use time-out as a discipline tool which is essentially an emotional punishment. When children are older and too big to drag to a corner, they use the disguised punishment called "consequences." Alfie Kohn, researcher on the effects of bribery and punishment calls "consequences" by the term "Punishment Lite." (Kohn, 1993) Parents use it as a punishment but call it a palatable euphemism under the word "consequences." We adults like to call it by name, but teens know better. They often have no choice in the matter because the adults decide how it is imposed. It is often a parent controlled device designed to hurt the child in order to teach a lesson.

Realistically, there are many consequences or outcomes to any choice but most consequences that parents force on children are hurtful and negative in some way. Even when there are multiple outcomes that will solve a problem (many of which are not hurtful or negative), parents still choose the one that will hurt a child in some way, in order to make the lesson or teaching stick. The problem is that it rarely teaches children to make better choices. Teens know that the parent is the one sticking it to them, and that they are not "choosing" the outcome, but the parent is imposing their outcome on them.

Health care professionals who promote the use of consequences forget one simple fact that every parent of teens know. Teens are humans. Teens have feelings, independent thought, and are in total control of the quality of their relationships that they choose to have-including a close relationship with a parent.

What is the outcome of "consequences?" There are three ways to solve any problem. Teens have the ability to push back and do. They can "leave" by shutting down all communication and basically shut the parent out. They can passively resist by using "attitude" and "snarkyness" or they can actively resist by engaging in behaviours which parents would rather they not engage in; drinking, drugs, vandalism and school failure. Some teens "surrender" to the consequences but suffer from internalizing conditions such as cutting, anxiety, eating disorders or depression.

I'm sure many teens would love to try "negotiating" with their parents instead of imposed consequences, but many parents refuse because of the false belief that one just doesn't "negotiate" in parenting.

Consequences have no place in any love relationship whether between partners or parent-child. Imposing a hurtful consequence on another person is not respectful. If you want an open relationship with your teen, you have to earn their respect, by showing respect for their feelings and dignity, and expecting that respect from them in return. If you wouldn't give your partner, or friend, or neighbor, or sister-in-law a consequence, why would you give your child one? They are human beings with real needs and feelings too. Respect is simply treating another human being as you would want yourself to be treated.

If you want to avoid teen rebellion, cancel the consequences. What to do instead? Use the "adult" method of solving any conflict; problem-solving and negotiation. Teach teens a valuable skill in getting along with others whether it's their boyfriend, boss, co-worker, coach or teacher. Learn how to resolve normative family problems so that everyone wins and have their needs met. Then, teach your teen how to do it. Practice together. There are many classes available to teach parents how to problem-solve with their child.

How to tell if your consequences are punitive or problem-solving

How to tell if consequences are punitive? If you threaten a certain outcome to get compliance, then it is being used as a punishment, which could invite a power struggle. If you come up with a "consequence" and insist on it, rather than getting input from your child on how to solve the problem, it's probably a punishment. If your child thinks it's a punishment, rather than a way to make amends or solve the problem, then it probably is a punishment! Ask your child for their opinion. Is the solution meant to hurt them or does it solve a problem? Is it the only way?

The best outcomes focus on teaching restitution, making amends, and solving problems. If a child spills a drink because she was careless pouring, she wipes up the mess. You would expect an adult to do the same. No further "consequence" is needed. A child who hits another child needs to be separated, calmed down, and told the rule. The restitution part might be to offer the other child a toy, hug, or an apology. If a child doesn't do his homework, no amount of taking away the cell phone is going to make him study and appreciate learning. Problem-solving with him about what the underlying issue is, will go further to uncover the true problem - is it boring? Too hard? He doesn't see the point in doing it? It's better to negotiate true solutions for the problem.

Look at the child's need or feelings

Here is another way to look at it. Your son rides his bike without a helmet – again. You've nagged, begged, pleaded, and informed him of the dangers of riding without. Next, you've issued "consequences!" You've taken the bike away and put it in the garage for a day, then a week, and then a whole month. You've done everything the parenting books say for a consequence to work. It's reasonable. Anyone can live a day without a bike. It's respectful. You're not hitting or calling him names. And it's related. No helmet, no bike. Simple to understand. But the problem is he is still riding a bike without a helmet! The situation could turn into a huge power struggle every time you take the bike away. Clearly, the consequence has not worked. Why not?

Consequences won't work, because the underlying need/feeling (NOF) of the child is not addressed. A child who consistently refuses to wear a bike helmet, even after having the bike locked away several times (and this is a common logical punitive consequence that parents take), may have a good reason for not wearing it. Perhaps he is being teased because it looks babyish. Maybe it's prickly or doesn't fit right. Active listening and mutual parent-child problem-solving are better tools used to uncover and address the underlying need.

Make sure outcomes are solution focused rather than pain focused. A common concern is, "Won't my child ever learn the consequences of his actions if I don't set up logical consequences? The more unpleasant the better?" Of course, he will. The rest of the world will be happy to teach your child the consequences of his actions. Teachers, coaches, other parents, bosses will be happy to give your child time-outs, punishments, detentions, withdrawal of privileges, and other consequences. Sometimes, it will be painful and inconvenient for him, but only you, the parent, can provide the safe haven of your loving relationship to teach him how to solve problems, make restitution, and amends. That's the harder job. The outside world is too busy to teach him those. You can! And the bonus is you'll enjoy less power struggles and more connection in your relationship. Only you, as their loving parent, have the incentive to spend time on negotiation with your child and teaching him lifelong, respectful relationship skills.

You are in the final third of parenting when you have a teen in the house. This is your last chance to teach your child a useful adult skill: problem-solving. Don't miss the opportunity.

Benefits of problem-solving

- Uses the wisdom and experience of the teen, as well as of the parent.

- Only the process needs consistency, not the outcomes. Outcomes are flexible enough to meet everyone's needs.

- When everyone participates in making rules, the rules are more likely to be respected.

- Parent's and child's needs are deemed equally important, and both are met.

- Everyone feels listened to, loved, and respected.

- Teens and adults get practice in problem-solving, brainstorming, and creative thinking skills. These soft skills are essential for success in today's world.

- The method strengthens relationships by facilitating growth, good feelings and intimacy.

- The method allows parents and child to deal with conflict rather than avoid it.

- It doesn't require the use of power, bribes, or punishment.

- It's not a compromise, which is still half-win, half lose. Both parent and child would have to give something up to get needs half met. Problem-solving allows both parent and child to have needs fully met by focusing on needs and not positions.

- The child learns self-discipline and responsibility.

- Problem-solving enables children to work out their conflicts respectfully with siblings and friends which is great training ground for all future relationships. (Gordon, 2011)

So cancel the consequences and treat your teen like the adult they almost are. Problem-solve any conflicts and begin to enjoy an adult relationship with your soon-to-be best friend!

Children react to punishment in the following three ways

Fight—They put up resistance, defiance, rebellion, and get even. They express anger and resentment. This is the most common reaction to punishment from spirited-temperament children.

Flight—They avoid communication and companionship with adults and may leave in various ways such as fantasy, daydreaming, alcohol, other drugs, and any other means of escape. Tuning out is one. Shying away out of fear is another way of avoiding parents.

Submit—They are compliant and follow rules and directives without any question, either from adults or peers. They become passive, dependent followers of anyone.

What should I use instead?

Discipline for Children ages 0-3 (Little self-control)	Discipline for Children ages 4 and up (Gaining self-control)
Supervision, childproofing, and prevention	Offer choices
Routines	Problem-solving and negotiation
Alternatives to "no" such as "later," "not today"	Make it a game
Substitution, distraction, and redirection	Teaching, listening and conversations
Acknowledge feelings (Active listening)	Natural safe consequences
I-statements	Acceptance (It's a stage)
Model appropriate behaviour	Also discipline tools for ages 0-3 in the left column
Give attention	Stay with your "No!"
Ignore "annoying" behaviour such as whining	Decide what your limits are and stick to them
Carry, pick up, or move them	

For a more comprehensive examination of the problems of punishment and thousands of tips on how to solve everyday misbehaviours of children from ages one to twenty, see the book, *Discipline Without Distress: 135 Tools for Raising Caring, Responsible Children Without Time-Out, Spanking, Punishment or Bribery*, by Judy Arnall (Professional Parenting Canada).

Sibling Anger

"Parents are not interested in justice, they are interested in quiet."
~ Bill Cosby, Actor

Siblings should be allowed to be angry with other. It's a natural component of living with someone. However, they need to be taught how to express and manage that anger respectfully. Children are not born knowing how to say I-statements and how to problem solve. They need to learn and you are the best person to teach them as you have a vested interest in their long-term relationship abilities. Discourage sarcasm, physical aggression, and name-calling, which is not productive. Give siblings the words of "I feel angry when you take too long on the computer, because I don't have enough time to play before I go out." This is more productive than the child saying, "Get off, stupid head; I want a turn!"

The more children practice I-statements with each other and to you, the more they develop the language of respectful communication when expressing anger to their future partner, bosses, mother-in-law, and the many other people in their lives.

How to handle sibling anger

1. Stay calm yourself
2. Get each of them calm

If children are physically or emotionally fighting, separate them. Try to calm each child before any problem-solving is done. As the mom of five, I know this is hard to do, but chances are, conflicts are usually between two children at a time. Wait it out. Distract them with some of the calm-down tools in Step 2. One of the best tools is to take each by the hand and have them sit down on either side of the sofa with you. Start reading out loud from a storybook. This builds their vocabulary and reading skills, allows everyone time to calm down and distracts them from their anger and conflict for a while. If you hate reading aloud, put on a bit of a movie or music to distract them. When everyone is ready, stop reading or stop the movie and start talking.

3. Help them solve the problem

Acknowledge the feelings and a bit of the situation of each child in front of the other child. "Aiden, you seem angry because you want a turn on the Xbox and Hanna won't give you one." "Hanna, you are frustrated because Aiden is pestering you for a turn, and you are trying to get up a level with the clock running." Help them formulate their feelings in an I-statement. "Aiden, here is how to say what you want. Say, 'I feel angry because I want a turn and you are ignoring me.'" "Hanna, you say, 'I'm frustrated from the game not going right, and now I'm feeling pressured to give it up.'" In this exchange, both are right and have valid feelings, but are taught how to communicate their unhappiness in a manner that is direct and respectful. I-statements are the most respectful confrontation language that adults use. You are teaching them another valuable life-long skill.

Next, move into problem-solving. "What are some ways we can solve this problem?" It really helps to put the game or fought-over toy on hold temporarily while conversing to solve problems. The kids are usually anxious to get back to playing and it will speed up the process.

There are other ways to work out conflicts, but each must agree to the process. Even when they agree, they may still end up angry if they lose.

Other ways to work it out

- Generate class, family, and group "rules" for everyone to follow
- Use the "Rock, paper, scissors" game to determine who goes first
- Pick a number from one to ten
- Put names and ideas in a hat and draw one
- Flip a coin with "heads" or "tails" determining the outcome
- Put "Reserved" or name cards on fought over items according to a schedule
- The "Bigger person" button is awarded to the child who gives something up
- Time schedules, sign-up sheets, and contracts are really helpful
- Give tokens for time slots
- Use the "Suggest and reject volley;" one person suggests and if the other person rejects, then they have to come up with a suggestion. This could go on for a long time!
- Have one child offer a more desired alternative in exchange to get what they want

Playdate Altercations

Playdates are not exempt from displays of anger when two or more children get into a tousle. Although conflict can occur anywhere, playdate disputes can be embarrassing for the parents and not very pleasant for the children either.

When your child is the hitter

You are having a lovely chat with a friend that you haven't seen in ages, when suddenly you hear a loud thud, an ear-piercing scream, and then another mother appears before you clutching a sobbing preschooler. Your son hit her daughter and now the mother and daughter and all eyes from the playgroup are on you as to what you are going to do about it. It's a parent's worst moment and one that is rarely covered in the parenting books. What is the best way to handle playgroup altercations that leaves everyone feeling content and validated?

Here are six easy steps:

Calming down

1. Comfort the other child if her parent is not around. Attend to any first aid necessary.

2. Ask for her point of view of what happened. If the parent is confronting you, listen carefully without interruption or judgment. Clarify any misunderstandings by asking questions. Validate her feelings even if you don't agree that the situation happened as she describes. This reduces her defensiveness. You could say, "It is very annoying to watch your child being hit."

3. Say that you need to talk to your child and you will be back.

4. Give your child the same opportunity to talk and listen without interruption and judgment. Children have an innate sense of fairness and can often tell you what preceded the altercation. Remember that your child might be upset too and you have to help him calm down. Validate his feelings of anger or frustration. Say, "You were angry that she took your truck?"

Restitution

5. When everyone is calm, go back to the other parent and her child and see if your child is ready to apologize. If he is, that's great. If he isn't, don't force it. It doesn't matter who is right or who is wrong as most altercations involve fault from both children. Ideally, both children should apologize to each other, but it rarely happens. You are concerned only with teaching your own child social manners. Model the act of apologizing by saying it yourself, such as "I'm sorry that my son hit your daughter. We will deal with it." This is all the other parent needs to hear. She has her "social bandage" – the apology, and your assurance that you will follow through with your child. You are not telling her how you will "deal with it" and that's okay. Modeling an apology shows your child how to make amends but respects his emotional status by not forcing him to do it when he is clearly not in that mindset yet. Sometimes the situation demands immediate apologies because of time constraints, but children are not emotionally ready to do so yet. If that's the case, then your apology for your child's behaviour should suffice.

Follow-up

6. Here is the "We will deal with it" part. Do not punish your child! Away from the crowd and staring eyes, help him to discover techniques for handling his

anger other than hitting. Walking away, breathing, and counting to ten are all ways to handle anger that even a three-year-old can handle. Remember that you will show them these feeling management techniques many times. Assure your child of your unconditional love and your expectations that he will make a better choice the next time he is angry during playgroup. Supervise him closely. Nothing gets a group of parents more angry than dealing with a parent who ignores her child's aggressive behaviour among their children.

If another conflict ensues with the same child or another child, recognize that your child is having a bad day and go home. Have some cuddle time and one-on-one attention time because perhaps that is what your child needs most of all. Don't forget to give yourself some pampering too! You are an excellent parent dealing with a challenging day.

When your child is the victim

You hear a loud thud, an ear-piercing scream, and then your child appears before you with tear-stained cheeks and red eyes and is pointing to another child. Your son was hit by another parent's daughter in the playgroup and you are wondering what to do. The mother is busy chatting away to another parent and is missing the entire scenario. What is the best way to handle this type of playgroup altercation?

Here are six easy steps:

Calming down

1. Comfort your child. Attend to any first aid necessary. Acknowledge his feelings. Say, "You are sad and hurt because you were hit." Wait until he is done crying. Keep comforting him until he is fully calm and able to listen to you. Ask him what had happened and what he would like to occur. Remember to stay calm yourself!

Restitution

2. Find the other child if she is still present. The first rule of conflict resolution is to speak to the person directly responsible for the negative feelings. That would be the other child, not the parent. Go to the child and encourage your child to speak about how he feels over what happened and what action he would like to have. Perhaps he wants his toy back or wants his turn on the ride-on toys. He may even want an apology. Focus on what your child wants, not what the other child did. If you child is too shy to speak, you can do it for him. This teaches him the words and tone to use.

3. If the other child does nothing, the next step is to appeal to their parent. Again, speak in terms of how your child feels or what he wants, not how bad the other child's actions were. You could say, "My son was hit by your daughter when she took away his truck. Would it be possible for him to continue his turn with it?"

Follow-up

4. Hopefully, the parent will take control of the situation and your child will get the truck back. No matter how the child and parent react to you and your son's requests, you have three choices:

Surrender and redirect – Steer your child to another activity, ignore the other mom and her child and enjoy your day. Say to yourself and your child, "Oh well, what else can we play with?" This might be a good choice if the other child or parent is no longer present.

Leave – Leave the group for the day. This is a viable option if you just don't have the energy to deal with the other parent or if an altercation has happened more than once that day.

Negotiate – Continue to verbally assert your needs higher up the chain of command, such as appealing to the playgroup organizer. In conflict resolution, if the problem is not resolved at the level of the people directly involved, move up to people higher on the authority ladder. This shouldn't be the first step. Try to resolve things with the child first and then the other parent, because it's respectful to bring the problem to their attention first. Only appeal higher if there is no effort to resolve things from the daughter and her parent.

Order of Conflict Resolution

This begins with the children first.

Child to child (with parent coaching behind the scenes). If there is no resolution...
Parent to other child, then...
Parent to other parent, then...
Parent to administrators. If still not resolved, your choices are to surrender and let it go, or leave.

5. While playing with your child, or even on the ride home, debrief by asking him how he feels about the outcome and what he could do differently next time. This gives him a chance to vent and also to feel in control of his actions, even if he can't control the other child's actions.

6. Many parents feel that they need to teach the other child a lesson. This is not advisable. The other child is a product of her parents. You are not in charge of her life lessons. Focus on your child.

If another conflict ensues with the same child or another child, recognize that your child is having a bad day and go home. Have some snuggling and one-on-one time, because your child needs to feel comforted by his parent and shown that his feelings matter. It gives him the message that even though there are challenging people out there, we feel better by immersing ourselves with people that are kind and nurturing to ourselves. Don't forget to give yourself some pampering too! You are also an excellent parent dealing with a challenging day.

Partner Anger

"Setting a good example for children takes all the fun out of middle age." ~William Feather, Author

The parenting partnership is one relationship where children get to watch anger in action! All couples have conflict, but certain stages of the relationship can cause more sensitive times than others. Parenting babies, toddlers, and preschoolers can use up a lot of patience, and when things go wrong or we are just plain exhausted, our partners are a handier target than our children, because they are there and they are adults who can supposedly handle it. However, anger can wear down and erode a relationship if not handled with care.

Relationships thrive and grow with three things: kindness, forgiveness, and commitment. Try to treat your partner with the kindness you readily give strangers in a store, or even the kindness you give your children. Polite, warm comments and communication keep love alive. Forgiveness is important because no one is perfect. We all mess up. We may express anger without care and hurt our partners, and being able to apologize and forgive is essential. Commitment to do better in the future and give more effort to our relationship is what keeps us in the game for the long haul.

We need to use I-statements with our partners when we are angry. "I'm angry that you are driving too fast and worry that we might skid off the road in these conditions." We need to actively listen to our partner's defensiveness, such as, "You are angry and feel that I am criticizing your driving." We need to solve the problem, "We have a conflict here and I am hoping we can come to some mutual solution." We also need to apologize if we have been less than kind. "I'm sorry for yelling at you while you were steering. I should have used a more respectful tone."

We need to demonstrate these skills *in front* of the children. Children are very well versed in watching parents fight and in using You-statements such as, "You never drive safely when I'm in the car!" They see us get angry and sulk, or hurl sarcasm at our partners, yet they don't get to watch how a couple initiates discussion again.

Children need to learn how to start a conversation flowing, after a conflict, and how to resolve future issues by engaging in problem-solving, as well as how to apologize by watching how their parents do this with each other. Respectful anger resolution is essential for children to learn by watching the best model available-their parents. They won't see it by watching media.

Get yourself calm by time-out. Get your partner calm by time-in. Solve the problem by talking together. Making up in front of the children shows them that open communication and respectful communication grows relationships and doesn't hurt them. Respectful but honest partners can handle normal conflict.

CONCLUSION

The Best Parenting Moments

As a parent educator, I experience a lot of parenting problems revealed in groups and workshops, and sometimes it's necessary to look at the many little joys of parenting, not so much in taking trips to Disneyland® or going to the zoo. It's the little insignificant moments that are wonderful, fleeting, and keeps us motivated in nurturing, loving, and parenting our children. So here is my list.

Labour is worth it when…

As babies

- Their little heads snuggle under your chin, and you can stroke their round little warm bodies swaddled in cloth.
- They smell so sweet after baths and sleeping.
- Their first smile breaks across their face as they recognize YOU!

As toddlers

- When they sleep in those padded-feet sleepers and they're lying on their tummies and their bum is up in the air. (How can anyone sleep that way?)
- When they raise their arms to you (and say, "up, up") and only you will do.
- When your child says, "I love you, Mommy!" for the first time.
- When your child gazes at the moon as she really looks at it for the first time with total wonder.
- When his sticky face has a ring of chocolate circling around his lips, under his nose and around his chin.

As preschoolers

- When your preschooler wants his new little playmate for a sleepover and you remind him that he needs to get out of the family bed first.

- When your child emphatically tells his playmates the "house rules" that he never "listens to" himself.

- When you get to wear mother-daughter dresses and your daughter is so proud of you.

- When you're all outside playing, the weather is gorgeous, and your children are getting along famously.

As school-agers

- When your school-aged child takes a moral stand against his peers.

- When she learns a new concept and gets that "ah-ha" look in her eyes.

- When your daughter and you share days at the spa, trade each other's clothes, take car-repair workshops, and share tissues while watching chick flicks together.

- When you have a disagreement with your partner and your child comforts you with hugs, tissues, and loving words.

As teenagers

- When they take great glee in correcting your bad driving habits because they learned the "correct way" in their driver's education course, despite the fact that you've been driving for thirty years with no collisions.

- When your six-feet-tall sons carry in the groceries, mow the lawn, take out the recycling, shovel the walk, repair the fence, unplug the toilet, and rebuild the basement.

- When the same sons actually clean the toilet!

- When your daughter walks to the store for groceries and cooks.

- When your older children comfort your younger children in the way you used to comfort them and you realize that they can carry on without you someday and do just fine.

- When you gain your life back in increasingly faster steps as they get more independent every day, and with the added joy of considering your children to be your closest friends.

- When you can sit around the table and play board games, laugh, joke, and have meaningful discussions on all topics of life.

- When you realize that yes, it was all worth it.

As adults

- When you look back at all the mistakes you made and realize how resilient children really are.

- When your "child" takes you to dinner and pays for it.

- When they move all their stuff with them as they leave home.

- When you are proud of not just their educational attainments, but who they have become as people.

- When you not only have your children as close friends, but they add the joy of grandparenting to your life and you get to experience all the wonderful moments of childhood again. "Remember when you used to…" becomes your most common phrase.

Aim for Excellence, not Perfection

 "At any given time, each of us is struggling with something that no one else knows about. Give everyone a break." ~ Anonymous

Anger is a useful, positive emotion when we can manage it effectively. All it takes is practice. Don't worry about the past. Begin again today. Every day that you don't yell or lash out is a positive step! We all have better days than others and no one is perfect. So stop trying to be. Remember to try to aim for calmness 70% of the time and you are doing excellently! Parenting young children is the hardest job in the world. If you can control your anger most of the time, help them learn to control their anger, and work together to solve the myriad of family issues, conundrums, and problems, you will be raising a child with valuable life skills in getting along with other people.

If you have yelled too much, or spanked, or used too many punishments in anger, then start clean today. Children are very forgiving. Above all, forgive yourself. Tell your children you are sorry and you are going to change things. Research shows that as parenting style changes, relationships can also turn around. (NLSCY, 2002-03) As children grow, you will find the instances of anger lessen as they grow more capable into fun and caring people that you will be proud to call your best friends.

Most of all, remember that you are the best, most important, and caring person in the world for your child. No one else can love and cherish your child as much as you do. Your children need you as their parent and they will love you forever, no matter what. Be kind to yourself and be the person you want them to be. Be kind and supportive to other parents because no one knows how hard sometimes parenting can be as well as other parents do. At any given time, we are each dealing with something on our plates that no one else is privy to. Let's cut each other some slack. We are all in this wonderful land of raising the next generation together. Be kind and support your parenting partner who is your team player in this game of love. No one is perfect, but we can aim for excellence!

Best wishes,

Judy Arnall
Former yelling parent and current parent of three young adults and two teens.

REFERENCES

Introduction

Stout, Hilary, October 21, 2009, "For Some Parents, Shouting is the New Spanking," *New York Times,* New York, NY

Sutherland-Smith, Shannon, February 21, 2013 "No Use Ranting about Yelling," *Calgary Herald,* Postmedia News, Calgary, AB

Key Concepts: Toxic Stress, Center on the Developing Child, Harvard University, accessed May 1, 2013 http://developingchild.harvard.edu/key_concepts/toxic_stress_response/

Step 1

Neufeld, Gordon, PhD, and Gabor Mate, MD, 2004, *Hold On to Your Kids: Why parents matter,* Alfred A. Knopf, Toronto, ON

NLSCY - National Longitudinal Survey of Children and Youth, Social Development Canada and Statistics Canada, 1994-95, 2002-03, - ongoing study, Ottawa, ON

Baumrind, Diana, PhD, 1971, "Current Patterns of Parental Authority," *Developmental Psychology Monograph,* 4, 1-103. Pages 32, 462

Baumrind, Diana, PhD, 1967, "Child Care Practices Anteceding Three Patterns of Preschool Behavior," *Genetic Psychology Monographs,* 75, 1-103. Page 462

Arnall, Judy, 2014, *The Parenting Information Maze: How to find the advice that fits your family,* Professional Parenting Canada, Calgary, AB

"NLSCY - Parenting Style and Children's Aggressive Behaviour," *The Daily,* Statistics Canada, http://www.statscan.ca/Daily/English/041025/d041025B.html, Accessed November 2, 2004

Owens, Anne Marie, October 26, 2004, "Sparks Fly Over Punitive Parenting: Parents cause aggression, study says," *CanWest News Service,* Calgary Herald, Calgary, AB

Bowlby, John, 1988, *A Secure Base: Parent-Child Attachment and Healthy Human Development,* Tavistock professional book. London, UK

Barker, Leslie, Summer 2014, "Moms and Dads: Same love, different approach," by Terry Bullick, *Apple Magazine,* Alberta Health Services, Calgary, AB

Berk, Laura E., 2000, *Child Development,* 5th Edition, Pearson Education, Massachusetts, IL

Arnall, Judy, 2012, *Discipline Without Distress: 135 tools for raising caring, responsible children without time-out, spanking, punishment or bribery,* 4th Edition, Professional Parenting Canada, Calgary, AB

Crary, Elizabeth, 2003, *Dealing with Disappointment,* Parenting Press, Seattle, WA

Neufeld, Gordon, PhD, 2010, Keynote at Medicine Hat Parenting Conference, Medicine Hat, AB

Weininger, Otto, PhD, 2002, *Time-in Parenting,* Rinascente Books Inc, Toronto, ON

Gershoff, Elizabeth, T., PhD, Columbia University, 2002, "Corporal Punishment by Parents and Associated Child Behaviors and Experiences: A meta-analytic and theoretical review," *Psychological Bulletin* Vol. 128, No. 4, 539-579, American Psychological Association Inc., Washington, DC

Roan, Shari, September 24, 2009, "Spanking Children Linked to Lower IQ's", *Los Angeles Times,* Los Angeles, CA

Step 2

Tremblay, Richard, PhD and Willard W. Hartup, EdD, and John Archer, PhD, 2005, *Developmental Origins of Aggression,* The Guilford Press, New York, NY, Richard Tremblay is the Canadian Research Chair in Child Development at The University of Montreal.

McGinn, Dave, Oct 27, 2011 "Aggressive Children Aren't Born That Way" *The Globe and Mail,* Toronto, ON

American Psychiatric Association, (DSM-5), *Diagnostic and Statistical Manual of Mental Disorders,* 2013, Fifth Edition, American Psychiatric Publishing, Arlington, VA

Greene, Ross, W., PhD, 2010, *The Explosive Child,* Harper Collins, New York, NY

Armstrong, Thomas, PhD, 1999, *Seven Kinds of Smarts: Identifying and developing your multiple intelligences,* Plume, New York, NY

Fowler, Bree, December 26, 2013, "Experts Worry about Long-term Effects of Tablets on Kids," *Calgary Herald,* Calgary, AB

Sheedy Kurcinka, Mary, 2006, *Raising Your Spirited Child,* Harper, New York, NY

Sears, William, MD and Martha Sears, RN, 1996, *Parenting the Fussy Baby and High-Need Child,* Little, Brown and Company, Boston, NY

Step 3

Child Development Stages and Capabilities sources:

- Barker, Leslie, Editor, 2012, *Terrific Toddlers: A facilitators manual,* Alberta Health Services, Calgary, AB

- Barker, Leslie, and Terry Bullick, 2012, *Growing Miracles,* 4th Edition, Alberta Health Services, Calgary, AB

- Berk, Laura E., PhD, 2000, *Child Development,* 5th Edition, Pearson Education, Massachusetts, IL

- Bibby, Reginald W. PhD, 2001, *Canada's Teens: Today, yesterday, and tomorrow,* Stoddart Publishing Company Limited, Toronto, ON

- Boyd, Denise, and Paul Johnson, Helen Bee, 2012, *Lifespan Development,* 4th Canadian Edition, Pearson Education Canada Inc., Toronto, ON

- Durrant, Joan E., PhD, 2011, *Positive Discipline for Everyday Parenting,* 2nd Edition, Save the Children Sweden, Stockholm, Sweden

- Gray, Peter, PhD, 1994, *Psychology,* 2nd Edition, Worth Publishers, Boston College, Massachusetts, IL

Levy, Shawn, Director, 2010, *Date Night,* DVD

Thomas, David, October 13, 2013, "The Seven Stages of Marriage", *The Sunday Telegraph,* London, UK

Brown, Susan, and I-Fen Lin, March 2013, *The Gray Divorce Revolution: Rising divorce among middle-aged and older adults,* 1990-2010, National Center for Family & Marriage Research Working Paper Series WP-13-03, Bowling Green State University, Bowling Green, OH

Date Night YYC, Professional Parenting Canada, http://datenightyyc.ca, Accessed June 1, 2014

Arnall, Judy, 2014, The Parenting Information Maze: *How to find the advice that fits your family,* Professional Parenting Canada, Calgary, AB

Gordon, Thomas, PhD, 2000, *Parent Effectiveness Training,* Crown Publishing, Random House, New York, NY

Kohn, Alfie, 1993, *Punished by Rewards: The trouble with gold stars, incentive plans, A's, praise and other bribes,* Houghton Mifflin Company, Boston, NY

Gordon, Thomas, PhD, 2011, *Teaching Children Self-Discipline,* Times Books, New York, NY

NLSCY - National Longitudinal Survey of Children and Youth, Social Development Canada and Statistics Canada, 1994-95, 2002-03, - ongoing study, Ottawa, ON

Parenting With Patience by Judy Arnall

APPENDIX

CALM-DOWN TOOLS TO CUT OUT

Are you a visual person?	
Watch an aquarium	Read a book
Draw	Visualize your happy place
Play video games	Record on a white board
Watch funny video clips	

Are you an auditory/verbal person?

Listen to music	Yell into the toilet
Dance and sing	Talk to a friend
Cry	Record your feelings
Silent scream	Scream at the wall
Hiss	Count to 10
Breathe	Drink water

Are you a creative person?

Write in a journal	Make poster of calm-down tools
Make a mad-meter	Work on a project
Draw a picture	Write a poem
Write a letter or email	Knit
Play Lego®	Make a model
Play a musical instrument	

Parenting With Patience by Judy Arnall

Are you a self-nurturing person?

Get a hug	Bubble bath
Make a calm-down corner	Drink water
Eat a healthy snack	Go out with friends
Be alone	Phone a friend

Are you a humorous person?

Make a joke	Read a funny book
Watch funny videos	

Are you a physical person?

Pillow scream	Squeeze stress balls
Play with Playdough®	Play with Lego®
Clean or vacuum	Knead bread
Weed or garden	Dance, rollerblade, bike, walk
Shake off feelings	Breathe
Stomp, run or jump	Bounce on a ball
Blow into an anger tube	Hug
Rip paper	Fuss box

Parenting With Patience by Judy Arnall

Are you a physical person?

Continued

Make faces at the wall	Drum
Bathe or shower	Play piano
Mow lawn, shovel walk	Hit a bop-bag or bean bag chair
Hang laundry or wring towels	Blow balloons or bubbles
Do recycling	Pick up clutter
Touch a button	Play with toys
Jump on the treadmill	

Parenting With Patience by Judy Arnall

My Anger Plan Worksheet

Accept—What are my trigger situations?

Neutralize—Tools I'm going to try to calm down in the moment

Get Away—Where and what is my time-out place?

Examine—What areas can I de-stress my life?

Return and resolve—What am I going to do?

My I-statement is:

I feel _____

when _____

because_____ .

I'm going to deal with this by:

Surrender

_____

or Leave

_____

or Negotiate/Collaborate/Problem-solve

_____

Parenting With Patience by Judy Arnall

Problem-solving Template

Problem:

Parent's Needs:	Child's Needs:

Ideas:
1.
2.
3.
4.
5.
6.
7.

Agreed Solution:
Check-back Date:

Parents' Quick Guide to Parenting Information

Parenting Style	Authoritarian	Authoritative
Parenting Goal	Control children	Control children. Teach thinking skills and self-control
Provides	High structure Low nurturing	High structure High nurturing
Decision Making	Parent	Parent > Child
Parenting Tools	Behaviour Modification (BM) strategies	BM (Light punishment) + Communication strategies
Expectations	Compliance	Relationship but with parent authority
Rule Making	Parent	Parent > Child Parent makes with child's input
Discipline	Rewards, physical punishments, emotional punishments and light punishments such as withdrawal of privileges.	Rewards, uses light punishments or emotional punishments such as logical consequences, jail time-outs, withdrawal of privileges and items. No physical punishment.
Programs and Resources	Any book, or program that advocates for spanking or physical punishment	Alfred Adler, Adlerian-based programs: Active Parenting, Systemic Training for Effective Parenting (S.T.E.P.), 123 Magic, Supernanny TV, Triple P (Positive Parenting Program), Rudolph Dreikurs, Love and Logic

Parents' Quick Guide to Parenting Information

Collaborative	Indulgent	Uninvolved
Influence children. Teach thinking skills and self-control	Control children No Teaching	No control or teaching
High structure High nurturing	Low structure High nurturing	Low nurturing Low structure
Parent = Child	Child > Parent	Child
Communication and Problem-solving	BM (Bribery) and Communication	None
Relationship with mutual respect	Relationship	None
Parent = Child Parent and child make together with age-appropriateness	Child > Parent	Child
Teaches, uses collaborative problem-solving, natural consequences and time-in. No punishment of any kind, physical or emotional, but does not tolerate bad behaviour.	Rewards heavily, shields from any punishments or natural consequences. No problem-solving as parents' needs not relevant.	No interaction at all.
Carl Rogers, Rogerian-based programs: P.E.T. Parent Effectiveness Training, How to Talk So Kids Will Listen and How to Listen So Kids Will Talk, Attachment Parenting, Positive Discipline (Durrant, and Nelson), Terrific Toddlers, Non-Violent Communication	Any book or program that doesn't advocate for age-appropriateness parent supervision and monitoring	

*Note - this is not an exhaustive list. This table is only meant as a guideline for parenting program philosophies. Parents are advised to make their own decisions regarding the best programs for their family's situation.

Also by Judy Arnall
Specialist in Non-Punitive Parenting

Order the 440 page world-wide bestseller of tips and tools to raise caring children from babies to teenagers without any kind of physical or emotional punishment. Comes with a handy chart of common misbehaviours and matching strategies.

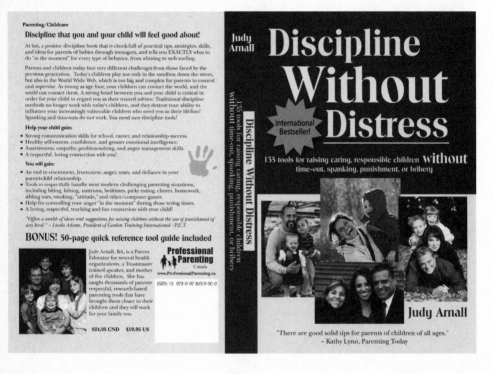

Available at Amazon, Kobo, Chapters Indigo, Barnes and Noble and most bookstores

Reclaim your parenting confidence!

This one-page parenting advice book is one of the most important pieces of advice that new and experienced parents will need in their parenting journey.

"Whenever I start doubting my parenting, I just open this book, and feel so much better." Maija Mills, BScPT

"This book is a wonderful tool to help parents trust their instincts and stay true to their own parenting beliefs!" Elizabeth Deneer-Roche, B.ChSt

"An essential gift for every new or experienced parent, for those times they feel judged, unappreciated or are just having a really bad day" Brenda Beatty, CBE, and mom of 5

"Finally, a book that tells you everything you REALLY need to know." Nicole Brouwer, BSc BEd, Parent Educator and mom of two

"My partner loved this gift." John Melisky

"A fantastic book that really encourages you to trust your instincts as a parent." Carolyn Campbell, Childbirth educator and mom of 4

"My Mother-in-law gave me this book when I became a new mom and I am forever grateful for this token of her support." Angela Farrell

Judy Arnall, BA, is a Parent Educator for several health organizations, a Toastmaster and professional speaker, and the best-selling author of "Discipline Without Distress: 135 Tools for Raising Caring, Responsible Children Without Time-out, Spanking, Punishment or Bribery," and "Plugged-In Parenting: Connecting with the Digital Generation for Health, Safety and Love." As the mother of five children, Judy has taught thousands of parents non-punitive, research-based parenting tools and skills that have enabled parents and children to build caring, close, and respectful bonds.

Professional Parenting
www.professionalparenting.ca

9780978050924

$12.95 $12.95

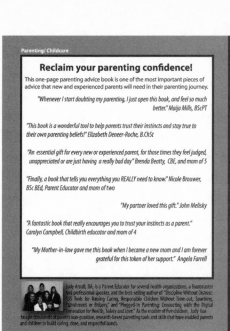

The Last Word on Parenting Advice

"The secret to confident parenting – in just one page"
-Teresa Pitman

Judy Arnall

Connect with your digital children while keeping them safe, healthy and happy!

Disc One - *Media is the Other Parent :* **74 minutes**

Family Trends- The Generation Gap Widens
6 major changes to family lifestyle since the electronic revolution
What is "screen time?"

Parenting Pointers- Parents Matter Most
5 essential pointers to keep kids connected and safe

Balance and Health
7 keys for a balanced life
4 warning signs of obsession

Parents' Fears and Children's Needs
8 fears of parents and 8 needs of children

Safety First
Entertainment Software Ratings Board (ESRB) codes
14 cyber-safety recommendations

Benefits of Internet and Gaming
20 academic, social and life-skill benefits of internet and video/computer games

Disc Two - *Teaching Digital Intelligence:* **51 minutes**

Babies and Toddlers 0-2yrs
Brain Development, Usage, Parents' Role, Safety Tips, How to Reduce Screen Time, and Experiential Learning

Preschoolers 3-5yrs
Development, Usage, Parents' Role, Safety Tips, How to Reduce Screen Time, Learning Styles, Acknowledging Feelings, Advertising, and Virtual Worlds

School-Agers 6-12yrs
Development, Usage, Parents' Role, Safety Tips, How to Reduce Screen Time, Sibling Fighting, Online Learning, Inactivity, Overeating, Cyber-bullying, Netiquette, Critical Thinking, Surveillance Programs and Luring Protection

Teenagers 13-19yrs
Development, Usage, Parents' Role, Safety Tips, How to Reduce Screen Time, One-time Consultation, Sharing Values, Boundaries, and Online Learning

Be a Part of Their World
The most important gift that children need and can't be provided virtually

Bonus! Includes 6 parenting vignettes showing problem-solving, acknowledging feelings and more!

Professional Parenting
©2010 Professional Parenting Canada
www.professionalparenting.ca
All rights reserved
ISBN 9780978050917

www.YouSpeakProductions.com
Cover design by PurpleWonda Creative

ISBN 978-0-9780509-1-7

125 minutes $34.95

Plugged-In Parenting

2 DVD Set

Connecting with the Digital Generation for Health, Safety and Love

Discipline Without Distress

By the author of Bestseller:

Judy Arnall

INDEX

INDEX

Conference Keynotes, Breakouts and Webinars Available
www.professionalparenting.ca

Keynotes:

Building a Three Pound Computer:™ How Parenting Affects Childhood Brain Architecture

Delete Your Distress: Mastering Work-life Balance in the Digital Age

Plugged-In Parenting: Connecting with the Digital Generation

Play is the Key to University

From Sand Comes Pearls: Helping Children Cope with Traumatic Events

Discipline Without Distress: 10 Essential Tools for the New Millennium

Parenting With Patience: Turn Frustration into Connection with 3 Easy Steps

To University from Unschooling: Why the Digital Generation Needs Adults More Than Content

Interactive Breakouts, E-Learning and Live Webinars:
All the above titles plus...

Alberta Health Services' Terrific Toddlers (four-week class)

Eggs for Dinner Again? Holding Down the Fort When Your Parenting Partner Works Away From Home

Communication Essentials: Conflict to Connection

Temperament Traits: Raising Your Spirited Child

Every Child is gifted! Understanding Multiple Intelligences

Taming the Gaming: How to Encourage Digital Intelligence

Run for your life! Taming Parent Anger

123 Time-Out: The Pros, Cons, and Alternatives

Self Esteem For Building a Better World

Ages and Stages: What to Expect When

Sleep Without Distress: Solving Your Family Sleep Problems

Mealtimes Without Distress: How to Solve Picky Eating Issues

Sleeping, Eating and Toileting: Turn Battlegrounds into Bonding Zones.

Brain Building Play Ideas

Sibling Rivalry Remedies

Harnessing Homework Hassles

Home-Schooling: Navigating the Sea of Choices.

Taming Temper: Handling Your Angry Child

He Dared Me! Helping Children Manage Peer Pressure.

Parenting Your Tween

Bully Busters: How to Help

Peaceful Partnering with Differing Parenting Styles

When Consequences, Spanking and Time-Out Don't Work

Your Promising Preschooler (four-week class)

Your Savvy School-aged Child (four-week class)

Your Tremendous Teenager (four-week class)

Dr. Thomas Gordon's Parent Effectiveness Training P.E.T. (six-week class)

Canadian Association of Professional Speakers

Judy Arnall, BA, DTM, CCFE

Conference Speaker, Trainer and Bestselling Author

Judy is an international award-winning professional speaker and a well-known Canadian education and parenting expert, who regularly appears on television interviews on CBC, CTV, and Global as well as publications including Chatelaine, Today's Parent, Canadian Living, Parents magazine, The Globe and Mail, Metro and Postmedia News.

As a Certified Canadian Family Life Educator (CCFE), Judy teaches family communication and parenting leadership at the University of Calgary, Continuing Education, and has taught for Alberta Health Services for 13 years. Judy founded the non-profit organization, Attachment Parenting Canada, which offers public courses and webinars across Canada. Judy is an authorized facilitator of the Parent Effectiveness Training (P.E.T.) series, and the Terrific Toddlers program, which she assisted in developing for Alberta Health Services.

As a conference keynote speaker, Judy will not read bullet points, and instead, engages audiences in interactive activities. Her keynote, *"Delete Your Distress: Mastering work-life balance in the digital age,"* is popular with corporations and associations. She is a professional member of CAPS (Canadian Association of Professional Speakers) and a DTM in Toastmasters.

Judy is the author of the worldwide bestseller, *"Discipline Without Distress: 135 Tools for raising caring, responsible children without time-out, spanking, punishment or bribery."* As a parent of five children, Judy has a broad understanding of the issues facing parents and the digital generation and has authored an educational DVD titled *"Plugged-In Parenting: Connecting with the digital generation for health, safety and love."* She is also the author of *"The Last Word on Parenting Advice," "To University From Unschooling,"* and *"The Parenting Information Maze: How to find the advice that fits your family."*

www.professionalparenting.ca   www.attachmentparenting.ca
jarnall@shaw.ca   (403) 714-6766

DATE DUE	